Beyond Malthus: Sixteen Dimensions of the Population Problem

LESTER R. BROWN, GARY GARDNER, AND BRIAN HALWEIL

Linda Starke, *Editor*

WORLDWATCH PAPER 143
September 1998

THE WORLDWATCH INSTITUTE is an independent, nonprofit environmental research organization in Washington, DC. Its mission is to foster a sustainable society in which human needs are met in ways that do not threaten the health of the natural environment or future generations. To this end, the Institute conducts interdisciplinary research on emerging global issues, the results of which are published and disseminated to decisionmakers and the media.

FINANCIAL SUPPORT for this research is provided by the David and Lucille Packard Foundation. Financial support for the Institute is provided by the Geraldine R. Dodge Foundation, the Ford Foundation, the William and Flora Hewlett Foundation, W. Alton Jones Foundation, John D. and Catherine T. MacArthur Foundation, Charles Stewart Mott Foundation, the Curtis and Edith Munson Foundation, Rasmussen Foundation, Rockefeller Brothers Fund, Rockefeller Financial Services, Summit Foundation, Surdna Foundation, Turner Foundation, U.N. Population Fund, Wallace Genetic Foundation, Wallace Global Fund, Weeden Foundation, and the Winslow Foundation. The Institute also receives financial support from the Friends of Worldwatch and from our Council of Sponsor members: Tom and Cathy Crain, Toshishige Kurosawa, Kazuhiko Nishi, Roger and Vicki Sant, Robert Wallace, and Eckart Wintzen.

THE WORLDWATCH PAPERS provide in-depth quantitative and qualitative analyses of the major issues affecting prospects for a sustainable society. The Papers are written by members of the Worldwatch Institute research staff and reviewed by experts in the field. Published in five languages, they have been used as concise and authoritative references by governments, nongovernmental organizations, and educational institutions worldwide. For a partial list of available Papers, see back pages.

Table of Contents

The views expressed are those of the authors and do not necessarily represent those of the Worldwatch Institute; of its directors, officers, or staff; or of its funding organizations.

ACKNOWLEDGMENTS: First, we would like to applaud the David and Lucille Packard Foundation for their strong and expanding population program. We would also like to thank Carl Haub, Karen Stanecki, Michael Hopkins, Robert Engelman, and Bob Young for thoughtful suggestions on preliminary drafts, and Joseph Chamie and Joseph Grinblat of the United Nations Population Division for providing key data as well as explanations of population projection methods.

We are grateful to our colleagues at Worldwatch for offering their expertise and criticism as the authors ventured into numerous research areas: Sandra Postel for fresh water, Ashley Mattoon and Janet Abramovitz for forests, John Tuxill and Chris Bright for biodiversity, Chris Flavin and Seth Dunn for climate change and energy, Anne Platt McGinn for oceanic fish catch, Michael Renner and Payal Sampat for jobs, and Hilary French for comments on the entire draft. We appreciate the enthusiastic support of Reah Janise Kauffman for the concept for the paper, for structural suggestions early on, and for coordination of the many drafts.

And for the work that only began once the writing had ended, we thank Dick Bell for strategic and thoughtful comments, Mary Caron and Amy Warehime for outstanding outreach, and Liz Doherty for flawless graphics and layout, and for her confidence that calms us all.

LESTER R. BROWN is founder, president, and a senior researcher at the Worldwatch Institute. The senior author of the Institute's two annuals, *State of the World* and *Vital Signs*, he is perhaps best known for his pioneering work on the concept of environmentally sustainable development.

GARY GARDNER is a senior researcher at the Institute and has written on agriculture, waste, and materials issues for the annual *State of the World* report, *World Watch* magazine, and other Institute publications.

BRIAN HALWEIL is a staff researcher and writes on issues related to food and agriculture, HIV/AIDS, cigarettes, and biotechnology.

Introduction: The Population Challenge

During the last half-century, world population has more than doubled, climbing from 2.5 billion in 1950 to 5.9 billion in 1998. Those of us born before 1950 are members of the first generation to witness a doubling of world population. Stated otherwise, there has been more growth in population since 1950 than during the 4 million years since our early ancestors first stood upright.[1]

This unprecedented surge in population, combined with rising individual consumption, is pushing our claims on the planet beyond its natural limits. Water tables are falling on every continent as demand exceeds the sustainable yield of aquifers. Eventual aquifer depletion will bring irrigation cutbacks and shrinking harvests. Our growing appetite for seafood has pushed oceanic fisheries to their limits and beyond. Collapsing fisheries tell us we can go no further. The Earth's temperature is rising, promising changes in climate that we cannot even anticipate. We are triggering the greatest extinction of plant and animal species since the dinosaurs disappeared. As our numbers go up, their numbers go down.

These effects of population growth are relatively recent, but assertions that population growth could affect human welfare are not. In 1798, Thomas Malthus, a British clergyman and intellectual, warned in his famous piece, *An Essay on the Principle of Population*, of the tendency for population to grow exponentially while food supply grew arithmetically. He saw a world where human numbers would

We gratefully acknowledge the financial support for this study from the David and Lucille Packard Foundation.

continually press against available food supplies.[2]

During the 200 years since Malthus issued his warning, famine has visited countries as diverse as Ireland and India, Ethiopia and China. Indeed, despite the near-tripling of the world grain harvest since 1950, the hungry and malnourished in 1998 number an estimated 840 million—nearly as many people as lived in the world when Malthus penned his essay.[3]

But the nature of famine has changed. Whereas it was once geographically defined by areas of poor harvests, today famine is economically defined by low incomes in those segments of society that lack the purchasing power to buy enough food. Famine concentrated among the poor is less visible than the more traditional version, but it is no less real. The World Health Organization (WHO) reports that 19,000 people, mostly infants and children, die each day from hunger and malnutrition.[4]

In addition to checks imposed by food shortages, there is evidence that other checks on population growth are now emerging, such as new infectious diseases, including AIDS. Ethnic conflicts within societies, such as Rwanda and the Sudan, are also taking a growing toll. Water shortages on a scale that would deprive people of enough water to produce food could undermine governments.

This study looks at 16 dimensions or effects of population growth in order to gain a better perspective on how future population trends are likely to affect the human prospect. The evidence gathered here indicates that the rapid population growth prevailing in a majority of the world's countries is not going to continue much longer. Either countries will get their act together, shifting quickly to smaller families, or death rates will rise from one or more of the stresses just mentioned. As human demands press against more and more of the Earth's limits, the question is not whether population growth will slow, but how. Will it be because countries do it humanely by shifting quickly to smaller families? Or because they fail to do so, and nature ruthlessly imposes its own constraints? In a world facing many challenges as it prepares to enter the next century, this may be the most challenging of all.

Estimates of future numbers are based on the latest United Nations population projections, using their medium-level figures. Under this scenario, world population will grow from 6.1 billion in 2000 to 9.4 billion in 2050—a gain of 3.3 billion. The other two U.N. projections put global population in 2050 as high as 11.2 billion or as low as 7.7 billion. While the medium scenario is judged by the U.N. demographers as the one most likely to materialize, it is not an inevitable population path for the next century. Indeed, because the projections are based exclusively on demographic assumptions and do not take into account the environmental limits to carrying capacity, they should be viewed as a first pass rather than the final word on estimates of future population.

We use the medium-level projections to give an idea of the strain this "most likely" outcome would place on ecosystems and governments, and the urgent need to break from the business-as-usual scenario. The mid-level projected growth in population of 3.3 billion by 2050 is very close to the growth that will have occurred between 1950 and 2000, some 3.6 billion. (See Table 1.) But there is one difference. During the half-century now ending, the growth occurred in both industrial and developing countries. During the next half-century, the entire burden of the projected increase of 3.3 billion will be in developing countries, many of which are hard-pressed to satisfy even existing demands on resources. In fact, the population of the industrial world is expected to decline slightly.[5]

The annual rate of world population growth reached its historical high in 1964 at 2.2 percent. Since then, it has been slowly declining, dropping to 1.4 percent in 1998. Despite the falling rate of growth, the number of people added each year increased from 72 million in 1964 to the all-time peak of 87 million in 1990. Since then, the annual addition has also declined, falling to 80 million in 1997, where it is projected to remain for the next two decades before starting to decline.[6]

The population projections for individual countries

TABLE 1

World Population, 1950, with Projections to 2050

Year	World Population	Half-Century Increase
	(billion)	
1950	2.5	
2000	6.1	3.6
2050	9.4	3.3

Source: See endnote 5.

vary more widely than at any time in history. At mid-century, populations were growing everywhere, but today they have stabilized in some 32 countries, while they continue to expand in some countries at 3 percent or more a year. Indeed, the world can be divided demographically into two camps: countries that have achieved population stability or are well on the way to doing so, and those that have not.[7]

With the exception of Japan, all the nations in the first camp are in Europe. And all are industrial countries. The populations of some countries, including Russia, Japan, and Germany, are actually projected to decline somewhat over the next half-century. In addition to the 32 countries, containing 12 percent of world population, that have stabilized their populations, in another 39 countries fertility has dropped to replacement level (roughly two children per couple) or below. Among the countries in this category are China and the United States, the first and third largest countries, which together contain 26 percent of the world's people.[8]

Although fertility in these 39 countries has fallen below replacement level, their populations have not yet stabilized because there is a disproportionately large number of young people moving into the reproductive age group. Thus even if they hold their fertility at replacement level, population may continue to grow for several decades before it stabilizes. It was this realization that led China nearly 20 years ago to shift its goal from a two-child to a one-child family. Leaders in Beijing realized that if they did not do this they would be faced with adding the equivalent of another India to their population—a development they considered potentially disastrous for their people.

In contrast to this group, some countries are projected to triple their populations over the next half-century. (See Table 2.) For example, Ethiopia's current population of 62 million will more than triple, as it climbs to 213 million in 2050. Pakistan's population is projected to go from 148 million to 357 million, surpassing that of the United States before 2050. Nigeria, meanwhile, is projected to go from 122 million today to 339 million, giving it more people in 2050 than there were in all of Africa in 1950. From an environmental vantage point, considering particularly the availability of water and cropland, it is unlikely that the projected population increases for these three countries, and other countries with similar projected gains, will materialize.[9]

As hard as it is to imagine the addition of another 3.3 billion people to the world's population, it is even more difficult to understand the effects of adding such numbers. As we look back over the last half-century, we see that world lumber use more than doubled, paper use increased nearly sixfold, grain consumption nearly tripled, water use tripled, and fossil fuel burning increased some fourfold. The relative contribution of population growth and rising affluence to the growth in demand for various resources varies widely. With lumber use, most of the doubled use is accounted for by population growth. With paper, in contrast, rising affluence is primarily responsible for the growth in use. For grain, population accounts for most of the growth, since consumption per person has risen only 30 percent since 1950. Similarly with water. For fossil fuels, the source of the growth in use is rather evenly divided between population growth and rising consumption.[10]

We have chosen to focus here on 16 dimensions of the population problem. Although we occasionally allude to the effect of rising affluence, no systematic effort is made to examine its consequences. Those interested in an analysis of the effect of rising affluence on the Earth's resources are

TABLE 2

The 20 Largest Countries Ranked According to Population Size, 1998, with Projections to 2050

Rank	1998 Country	Population (million)	2050 Country	Population (million)
1	China	1,255	India	1,533
2	India	976	China	1,517
3	United States	274	Pakistan	357
4	Indonesia	207	United States	348
5	Brazil	165	Nigeria	339
6	Pakistan	148	Indonesia	318
7	Russia	147	Brazil	243
8	Japan	126	Bangladesh	218
9	Bangladesh	124	Ethiopia	213
10	Nigeria	122	Iran	170
11	Mexico	96	The Congo	165
12	Germany	82	Mexico	154
13	Viet Nam	78	Philippines	131
14	Iran	73	Viet Nam	130
15	Philippines	72	Egypt	115
16	Egypt	66	Russia	114
17	Turkey	64	Japan	110
18	Ethiopia	62	Turkey	98
19	Thailand	60	South Africa	91
20	France	59	Tanzania	89

Source: See endnote 9.

urged to read an earlier Worldwatch book, *How Much Is Enough?*, by Alan Durning.[11]

One way to understand the consequences of future population growth is to contrast some of the key trends projected for the next half-century with those of the last one. For example, we have seen a near fivefold growth in the oceanic fish catch and a doubling in the supply available per person, but marine biologists now believe we may have "hit the wall" in oceanic fisheries and that the oceans cannot sustain a catch any larger than today's. Thus people born today are likely to see the catch per person cut in half during their lifetimes.[12]

Grainland per person has been shrinking since mid-century, but the drop projected for the next 50 years means the world will have less grainland per person than India has today. Future population growth is likely to reduce this key number in many societies to the point where they will no longer be able to feed themselves. Countries such as Ethiopia, India, Iran, Nigeria, and Pakistan will see grainland per person shrink by 2050 to less than one tenth of a hectare (one fourth of an acre)—far smaller than a typical suburban building lot in the United States.[13]

Given that the amount of fresh water produced each year is essentially fixed by nature, the water available per person has shrunk steadily as a result of population growth, leading to severe water shortages in some areas. Countries now experiencing these shortages include China and India, along with scores of smaller ones. As irrigation water is diverted to industrial and residential uses, the resultant water shortages could drop food production per person in many countries below the survival level. The fast-deteriorating water situation in India was described in July 1998 in one of India's leading newspapers, the *Hindustan Times*: "If our population continues to grow as it is now…it is certain that a major part of the country would be in the grip of a severe water famine in 10 to 15 years." The article goes on to reflect an emerging sense of desperation. "Only a bitter dose of compulsory family planning can save the coming generation from the fast-approaching Malthusian catastrophe."[14]

The challenge to governments presented by continuing rapid population growth is not limited to natural resources. It also includes education, housing, and jobs. During the last half-century, the world has fallen further and further behind in creating jobs, leading to record levels of unemployment and underemployment. Unfortunately, over the next 50 years the number of entrants into the job market will be even

greater. Few things threaten the political stability of a country as much as growing ranks of unemployed young people.[15]

As noted earlier, the U.N. population projections cited
here are based on exclusively demographic assumptions,
which are not related to the population carrying capacity of
local ecosystems. These projections are purely statistical,
based on historical data on fertility, mortality, and average
life span and assumptions about future trends. No effort was
made, for example, to determine the adequacy of water supplies for the projected populations. Updating and publish-
ing these projections is a vital service, but if their limitations
are not recognized and publicized, they can be misleading.
If they give the impression that projected population
increases are likely, when in reality life-support systems may
collapse long before they can materialize, they create a false
sense of security and lessen the urgency with which the population issue is addressed.

This paper sketches the stakes involved in another half-
century of population expansion. Based on the analysis in
it, we conclude that the medium projection of 9.4 billion
people in 2050, which U.N. demographers consider to be
the most probable, is unlikely to materialize. Rather, the
world is more likely to follow a path closer to the low population projection of 7.7 billion by mid-century.

What is less clear is whether we will move to the lower
trajectory because countries with rapid population growth
quickly shift to smaller families or because they fail to do so
and the resulting inability to manage threats from disease,
spreading hunger, or social disintegration leads to rising
death rates. In the concluding section, we return to the U.N.
population projections, assessing their feasibility.

Grain Production

The relationship between the growth in world population and the grain harvest has shifted over the last half-century, neatly dividing this period into two distinct eras. From 1950 to 1984, growth in the grain harvest easily exceeded that of population, raising the harvest per person from 247 kilograms to 342, a gain of 38 percent. (See Figure 1.) During the 14 years since then, growth in the grain harvest has fallen behind that of population, dropping output per person from its historic high in 1984 to an estimated 317 kilograms in 1998—a decline of 7 percent, or 0.5 percent a year.[16]

These global trends conceal widely divergent developments among countries, contrasts that can be seen for the world's two most populous nations: India and China. In both, grain production per person was close to 200 kilograms as recently as 1978. Since then, the figure in India has edged up slightly but still falls short of 200 kilograms, while in China production has surged since the economic reforms in 1978, with per-person output now at nearly 300 kilograms. The combination of a dramatic surge in grain production and an equally dramatic reduction in population growth has given China a large margin of safety, effectively eliminating most of its hunger and malnutrition. Meanwhile, although India has also achieved impressive gains in its harvest, these have been largely cancelled by population growth, leaving its 976 million people living close to the margin.[17]

What has happened in China and India is the story of developing countries in general. The overwhelming majority have achieved substantial, if not dramatic, gains in their grain harvests over the last half-century. Some, such as Thailand, have combined this with a much slower growth of population, which means that agricultural gains translate into rising grain production per person. In Pakistan, by contrast, grain production per person climbed steadily for awhile, but it peaked in 1981 at 186 kilograms. Since then it

World Grain Production Per Person, 1950–98

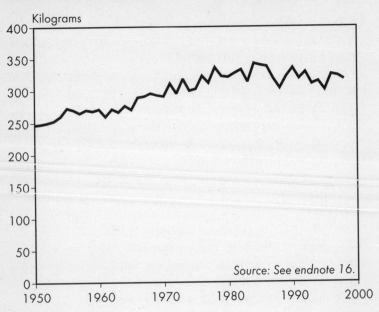

Source: See endnote 16.

has been declining nearly 1 percent a year. In effect, Pakistan's farmers are losing the battle with population growth.[18]

The slower growth in the world grain harvest since 1984 is due to the lack of new land and to slower growth in irrigation and fertilizer use. Irrigated area per person, after expanding by 30 percent from 1950 until 1978, has declined by 4 percent since then as growth in the irrigated area has fallen behind that of population.[19]

The increase in world fertilizer use has slowed dramatically since 1990, as diminishing returns to the application of additional fertilizer have stabilized use in the United States, Western Europe, and Japan and slowed annual growth in world fertilizer use from 6 percent between 1950 and 1990 to scarcely 2 percent in recent years.[20]

Although Malthus was primarily concerned with the additional demand for grain generated by population growth, rising affluence is also playing a role. In a low-income country such as India, grain consumption per person is less than 200 kilograms per year and diets are typically dominated by a single starchy staple—rice, for instance. With scarcely a pound of grain available a day per person, nearly all must be consumed directly, leaving little for conversion into animal protein. For the average American, on the other hand, the great bulk of the 800-kilogram daily grain consumption is taken in indirectly in the form of beef, pork, poultry, eggs, milk, cheese, ice cream, and yogurt. At the intermediate level, in a country like Italy, people consume 400 kilograms of grain a day. Future food price stability thus depends on expanding production fast enough to keep up with both population growth and rising affluence.[21]

One question often asked is, How many people can the Earth support? This must be answered with another question, At what level of consumption? If the world grain harvest of 1.87 billion tons were expanded to 2 billion tons in the years ahead, it would support 10 billion Indians or 2.5 billion Americans. To answer the question of how many people the Earth can support, we first have to know the level of consumption we expect to live at.[22]

Now that the frontiers of agricultural settlement have disappeared, future growth in grain production must come almost entirely from raising land productivity. Unfortunately, this is becoming more difficult. After rising at 2.1 percent a year from 1950 to 1990, the annual increase in grainland productivity dropped to scarcely 1 percent from 1990 to 1997. The challenge for the world's farmers is to reverse this decline at a time when cropland area per person is shrinking, the amount of irrigation water per person is dropping, and the crop yield response to additional fertilizer use is falling.[23]

Fresh Water

Wherever population is growing, the supply of fresh water per person is declining. As a result of population growth, the amount of water available per person from the hydrological cycle will fall by 74 percent between 1950 and 2050. Stated otherwise, there will be only one fourth as much fresh water per person in 2050 as there was in 1950. With water availability per person projected to decline dramatically in many countries already facing shortages, the full social effects of future water scarcity are difficult even to imagine. Indeed, spreading water scarcity may be the most underrated resource issue in the world today.[24]

Evidence of water stress can be seen as rivers are drained dry and as water tables fall. The Colorado River in the southwestern United States now rarely reaches the sea. The Yellow River, the northernmost of China's two major rivers, has run dry for a part of each year since 1985, with the dry period becoming progressively longer. In 1997, it failed to make it to the sea for 226 days. The Nile, the largest river in the Middle East, has little water left when it reaches the sea.[25]

Water tables are now falling on every continent, including in major food-producing regions. Among those where aquifers are being depleted are the U.S. southern Great Plains; the North China Plain, which produces nearly 40 percent of China's grain; and most of India. Wherever water tables are falling today, there will be water supply cutbacks tomorrow, as aquifers are eventually depleted.[26]

Some 70 percent of the water pumped from underground or diverted from rivers is used for irrigation, 20 percent is used for industrial purposes, and 10 percent is for residential use. Water use patterns vary widely by region. In Europe, for example, where agriculture is largely rainfed, water withdrawals are dominated by industrial use. In Asia, in contrast, irrigation accounts for 85 percent of all water use.[27]

As countries press against the limits of their water supplies, the competition among sectors intensifies. The economics of water use does not favor agriculture. One thousand tons of water can be used to produce one ton of wheat worth $200 or to expand industrial output by $14,000. This ratio of 70 to 1 explains why industry almost always wins in the competition with agriculture for water.[28]

As the growing demand for water collides with the limits of supply, countries typically satisfy rising urban and residential demands by diverting water from irrigation. They then import grain to offset the loss of irrigation water. Since it takes at least 1,000 tons of water to produce a ton of grain, importing grain becomes the most efficient way to import water. North Africa and the Middle East—a region where population growth is rapid and every country faces water shortages—has become the world's fastest-growing grain import market during the 1990s. In 1997, the water required to produce the grain and other foodstuffs imported into the region was roughly equal to the annual flow of the Nile River.[29]

In both China and India, the two countries that together dominate world irrigated agriculture, substantial cutbacks in irrigation water supplies lie ahead. The combination of the effects of aquifer depletion in key countries such as these and the growing diversion of irrigation water to nonfarm uses in many countries makes it unlikely that there will be much, if any, increase in total irrigated area over the long term. Already the irrigated area per person has been slowly declining since 1978, falling from a historical high of 0.047 hectares per person to 0.045 hectares in 1996—a drop of 4 percent. If the total irrigated area remains at roughly 263 million hectares until 2050, this key figure will fall to 0.028 hectares per person in 2050—declining by an additional 38 percent. (See Figure 2.) Such a shrinkage will pose a formidable challenge to the world's farmers. This dramatic worldwide decline in irrigated area per person meshes with a recent projection by Sandra Postel in *BioScience*, which concluded that by 2025 the additional irrigation water needed in world agriculture will be equal to the annual flow of 24 Nile Rivers.[30]

David Seckler and his colleagues at the International

FIGURE 2

Global Irrigated Area Per Person, 1950–96, with Projections to 2050

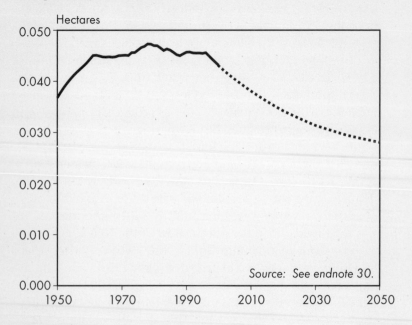

Source: See endnote 30.

Water Management Institute project that a billion people will be living in countries facing absolute water scarcity by 2025. These nations do not have enough water to maintain 1990 levels of food production per person from irrigated area, even with high irrigation efficiency, and to meet the needs for domestic, industrial, and environmental purposes as well. They will have to reduce water use in agriculture in order to satisfy residential and industrial water needs. The resulting decline in domestic food production will force them to import more food, assuming it is available. Although detailed water projections by sector for each country are not available for 2050, the number of water-deprived people will be far greater than in 2025 if the world continues on the U.N. medium population trajectory. The bottom line is that if we are facing a future of water scarcity, then we are also facing a future of food scarcity.[31]

Biodiversity

As human population has surged this century, the populations of numerous other species have tumbled, many to the point of extinction. Indeed, we live amid the greatest extinction of plant and animal life since the dinosaurs disappeared some 65 million years ago, with species losses at 100 to 1,000 times the natural rate. But humans are not just witnesses to a rare historic event, we are actually its cause. The leading sources of today's species loss—habitat alteration, invasions by exotic species, pollution, and overhunting—are all a function of human activities.[32]

A series of studies over the past decade by the World Conservation Union–IUCN has documented the stresses facing a broad range of species, with disturbing conclusions. Human activities have pushed the percentage of mammals, amphibians, and fish that are in "immediate danger" of extinction into double digits. (See Table 3.)[33]

The principal cause of species extinction is habitat loss—the result of encroachment by humans for settlements, for agriculture, or to claim resources such as timber. A particularly productive but vulnerable habitat is found in coastal areas, home to 60 percent of the world's population. Coastal wetlands nurture two thirds of all commercially caught fish, for example. And coral reefs have the second highest concentration of biodiversity in the world, after tropical rainforests. But human encroachment and pollution are degrading these areas: roughly half of the world's salt marshes and mangrove swamps have been eliminated or radically altered, and two thirds of the world's coral reefs have been degraded, 10 percent of them "beyond recognition." As coastal migration continues—coastal dwellers could account for 75 percent of world population within 30 years—the pressures on these productive habitats will likely increase.[34]

Habitat loss tends to accelerate with an increase in a country's population density. This is bad news for the world's "biodiversity hotspots"—species-rich ecosystems at

TABLE 3

Share of Species Worldwide Classified as Threatened

| | Share of Species That Is | | Total Share of Species Threatened with Extinction |
	In Immediate Danger of Extinction	Vulnerable to Extinction	
	(percent)		
Birds	4	7	11
Mammals	11	14	25
Reptiles	8	12	20
Amphibians	10	15	25
Fish	13	21	34

Source: See endnote 33.

greatest risk of destruction. Twenty-four of these hotspots, containing half of the planet's species, have been identified globally. Some of the most important hotspot countries will reach population densities that have been linked with very high rates of habitat loss. Five of the six most biologically rich countries (see Table 4) could see more than two thirds of their original habitat destroyed by 2050 if this historical relationship holds.[35]

Related to loss of habitat is the growing incidence of plant, animal, insect, and microbial invasions of ecosystems worldwide as human interchange increases. These "exotic species" sometimes dominate local ecosystems, eliminating native species and reducing overall diversity. Exotics are implicated in 68 percent of all fish extinctions in the United States this century, for example. Growth in human travel and commerce explains many accidental invasions by exotics, but foreign species are also deliberately introduced into farms, plantation forests, and aquaculture systems. Although only 1 percent of exotics cause widespread damage, exotic species are the second leading cause, after habitat destruction, of species loss worldwide.[36]

Other, often diffuse effects of expanded human activi-

TABLE 4

Population Density and Possible Habitat Loss, Countries of Major Importance for Biodiversity

	Population Density		Habitat Loss Historically Associated with Projected 2050 Population Density
	1995	2050	
	(number per square kilometer)		(percent)
Brazil	188	288	41
Madagascar	256	874	67
Mexico	478	807	67
Zaire	200	726	67
Colombia	345	600	78
Indonesia	1,090	1,757	85

Source: See endnote 35.

ties also disrupt ecosystems. Nitrogen, for example, is now made available to plants at more than twice the preindustrial rate as a result of fertilizer production, cultivation of nitrogen-fixing crops, and the burning of fossil fuels. This overfertilization of the Earth favors some species at the expense of others, leading to a reduction in diversity and resiliency of land and aquatic ecosystems.[37]

Likewise, greenhouse gas emissions could disrupt ecosystems on a vast scale. As with nitrogen, increased levels of atmospheric carbon may favor some species over others: annuals over perennials, for example, or deciduous trees over evergreens. To the extent that greenhouse gases induce changes in global climate, many species may be at risk as habitats shift or shrink, and as some life forms, such as insects or animals, adapt and migrate more quickly than others, such as plants. And as sea levels rise with a change in climate, ecosystems such as coastal wetlands could be destroyed.[38]

Climate Change

Over the last half-century, carbon emissions from fossil fuel burning expanded at nearly twice the rate of population, boosting atmospheric concentrations of carbon dioxide, the principal greenhouse gas, by 30 percent over preindustrial levels. (See Figure 3.) All major scientific bodies acknowledge the likelihood that climate change due to the buildup of greenhouse gases in the atmosphere is indeed under way. The 15 warmest years on record have all occurred since 1979, and 1998—based on the first seven months of data—is on target to surpass the 1997 high by a record margin. (See Figure 4.)[39]

The destabilization of our climate threatens more intense heat waves, more severe droughts and floods, more destructive storms, and more extensive forest fires. The relat-

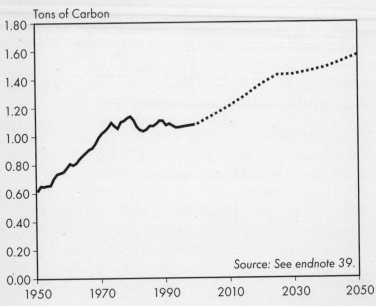

FIGURE 3

Global Carbon Emissions Per Person, 1950–95, with Projections to 2050

Tons of Carbon

Source: See endnote 39.

FIGURE 4

Average Temperature at the Earth's Surface, 1866–1998

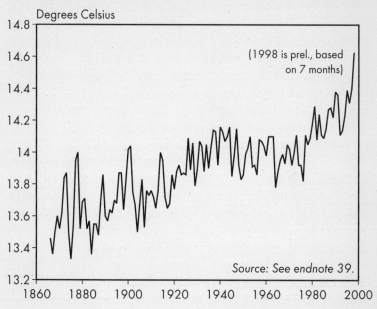

Degrees Celsius

(1998 is prel., based on 7 months)

Source: See endnote 39.

ed shifts in rainfall and temperature may jeopardize food production, the Earth's biological diversity, and entire ecosystems, as well as human health by expanding the ranges of tropical diseases. Unless efforts to curb them are stepped up, carbon emissions will continue to grow faster than population over the next 50 years, driving the Earth's climate system into unchartered territory. The Intergovernmental Panel on Climate Change (IPCC) estimates that an eventual two-thirds reduction in global emissions is needed to avoid precariously high levels of atmospheric carbon dioxide concentrations.[40]

The IPCC and the U.S. Department of Energy (DOE) project that emissions from developing countries will nearly quadruple over the next half-century, while those from industrial nations will increase by 30 percent. Although annual emissions from industrial countries are currently twice as high as from developing ones, the latter are on target to eclipse the industrial world by 2020.[41]

Higher per capita carbon emissions account for roughly 55 percent of the increase in emissions projected for developing nations. Emissions per person are due to more than double from 0.51 tons of carbon per year in 2000—just one fifth of the industrial level—to 1.14 tons in 2050. The remaining 45 percent of emissions increases is due to population growth.[42]

Fossil fuel use accounts for roughly three quarters of world carbon emissions. As a result, regional growth in carbon emissions tend to occur where economic activity, and related energy use, is projected to grow most rapidly. Emissions in China are projected to grow over three times faster than population in the next half-century, as emissions per person soar from 0.77 tons of carbon to 2.81 tons due to a booming economy that is heavily reliant on coal and other carbon-rich energy sources. In Africa, in contrast, emissions per person are expected to scarcely change—growing from the current level of 0.30 tons to 0.33 tons in 2050, despite a threefold increase in total emissions.[43]

The effects of population growth are most profound in countries where people are heavy emitters. For example, the 115 million people added to the population of the United States between 1950 and 1998—an increase of nearly 75 percent in just 45 years—account for more than one tenth of current global emissions. And the carbon emissions of the 75 million people who will be added to the U.S. population in the next 50 years roughly equal the emissions of the 1.3 billion people who will be added to Africa during that period.[44]

Deforestation and other land use changes account for the remainder of world carbon emissions. Forests have served as a sink for carbon throughout much of human history. In recent years, however, the world's forests have become net sources of atmospheric carbon, largely due to forest burning and clearing in the tropics. Six months of fires in Asia in 1997 and 1998 released more carbon than Western Europe emits from fossil fuel burning in an entire year. The carbon contribution from this source will likely increase in coming years as the burgeoning human population continues to cut down forests.[45]

Oceanic Fish Catch

From 1950 until 1988, the oceanic fish catch soared from 19 million to 88 million tons, expanding much faster than population. The per capita catch increased from less than 8 kilograms in 1950 to the historical peak of just over 17 kilograms in 1988, more than doubling. (See Figure 5.) Since 1988, however, growth in the catch has slowed, falling behind that of population. Between 1988 and 1996, the catch per person declined to less than 16 kilograms, a drop of some 9 percent.[46]

This fivefold growth in the human appetite for seafood since 1950 has pushed the catch of most oceanic fisheries to their sustainable limits or beyond. Marine biologists believe that the oceans cannot sustain an annual catch of much more than 93 million tons, the current take.[47]

As we near the end of the twentieth century, overfishing has become the rule, not the exception. Of the 15 major oceanic fisheries, 11 are in decline. The catch of Atlantic cod—long a dietary mainstay for West Europeans—has fallen by some 70 percent since peaking in 1968. Since 1970, bluefin tuna stocks in the West Atlantic have dropped 80 percent.[48]

The next half-century is likely to be marked by the disappearance of some species from markets, a decline in the quality of seafood caught, higher prices, and more conflicts among countries over access to fisheries. Over the last two decades, a growing share of the catch has consisted of inferior species, some of which were not even considered edible in times past.[49]

The growing scarcity of the species at the top of the food chain is reflected in rising prices. Poor people who once ate fish because they could not afford meat now find that meat is often less expensive than seafood. Although most price rises are moderate, some are extreme—going far beyond anything we could have earlier imagined. The decline of the bluefin tuna population in the Atlantic, for instance, has occasionally pushed prices for a 300-kilogram tuna above

FIGURE 5

World Fish Catch Per Person, 1950–96, with Projections to 2050

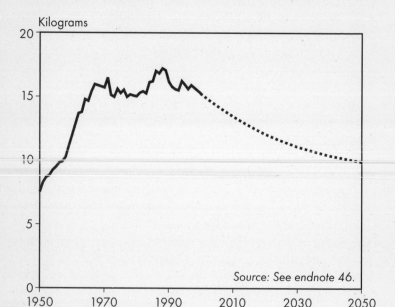

Source: See endnote 46.

$80,000 as top-of-the-line sushi restaurants in Japan compete for the few of these giant fish that are available.[50]

This growing competition for limited resources has led to ongoing conflicts among countries. The United Nations recorded more than 100 such disputes in 1997. These are evident in the cod wars between Norwegian and Icelandic ships, between Canada and Spain over turbot off Canada's eastern coast, between China and the Marshall Islands in Micronesia, between Argentina and Taiwan over Falkland island fisheries, and between Indonesia and the Philippines in the Celebes. A Greenpeace spokesperson notes there are "tuna wars in the northeast Atlantic, crab wars in the North Pacific, squid wars in the southwest Atlantic, salmon wars in the North Pacific, and pollock wars in the Sea of Okhotsk." Although these disputes make it into the world news only rarely, they are now an almost daily occurrence. Indeed, historians may record more fishery conflicts during one year in the 1990s than during the entire nineteenth century.[51]

One of the consequences of modern fishing technologies, whether it is the use of drift nets or bottom-scouring fishing techniques, is an increase in the bycatch—the inadvertent catch of unwanted species. This oceanic equivalent of clear-cutting is damaging fisheries on an unprecedented scale.[52]

With the oceans now pushed to their limits, future growth in the demand for seafood can be satisfied only by fish farming. As a result, aquacultural output has increased from 7 million tons in 1984 to an estimated 26 million tons in 1997. Most of this growth in catch is based on just a few species, such as carp, which constitute most of the aquacultural harvest in China, and catfish, which dominates fish farming in the United States. As the world turns to fish farming to satisfy its needs, fish begin to compete with livestock and poultry for feedstuffs such as grain, soybean meal, and fishmeal.[53]

Given that the oceanic fish catch is apparently now at or beyond its sustainable limit, it is a relatively simple matter to determine the future oceanic catch per person. With each year, this will decline by roughly the amount of population growth, dropping to 9.9 kilograms per person in 2050, a decline to little more than half the 1988 peak of 17.2 kilograms. Those of us born before 1950 have enjoyed a doubling of the seafood catch per person, while those born in recent years are likely to witness a decline of nearly one half during their lifetimes.[54]

Jobs

Since mid-century, the world's labor force has more than doubled—from 1.2 billion people to 2.7 billion, outstripping the growth in job creation. As a result, the United Nations International Labor Organization estimates that nearly 1 billion people, approximately 30 percent of the global work force, are unemployed or underemployed (working but not earning enough to meet basic needs). Over the next half-century, the world will need to create more than 1.9 billion jobs—all of them in the developing world—just to maintain current levels of employment.[55]

As economists often note, while population growth may boost labor demand (through economic activity and demand for goods), it will most definitely boost labor supply. During the next 50 years, almost 40 million people will enter the global labor force—defined as those between the ages of 15 and 65 seeking work—each year. Between 1995 and 2050, some 1.9 billion additional jobs will need to be created to absorb these new would-be workers. (See Table 5.) The most pressing needs will be found in the world's poorest nations—a sobering example of the vicious cycle linking poverty and population growth.[56]

As the children of today represent the workers of tomorrow, the interaction between population growth and jobs is most acute in nations with young populations. Nations such as Peru, Mexico, Indonesia, and Zambia with more than half their population below the age of 25 will feel the burden of this labor flood. In the Middle East and Africa, 40 percent of the population is under the age of 15. Since new entrants into the labor force were born at least 15 years ago, measures to reduce population growth have a delayed effect on the growth of the labor force, highlighting the urgency of taking action on population.[57]

Nowhere is the employment challenge greater than in Africa, where at least 40 percent of the population lives in absolute poverty. Although 8 million people entered the sub-

TABLE 5

World Labor Force, 1995, with Projections to 2050

	1995	2050	Additional Jobs Required, 1995 to 2050	Change, 1995 to 2050
		(million)		(percent)
World	2,735	4,666	1,932	71
Industrial Countries	598	509	-88	-15
Developing Countries	2,137	4,157	2,020	94
Least Developed Countries*	261	945	684	262

*28 poorest nations in the world, based on per capita GNP.
Source: See endnote 56.

Saharan work force in 1997, by 2030 this resource-scarce region will have to absorb more than 17 million new entrants each year. Over the next half-century, Nigeria's labor force is projected to grow by 246 percent and Ethiopia's will soar by 337 percent—both faster than growth of the general population. At current growth rates, the size of the labor force in sub-Saharan Africa will more than triple by 2050.[58]

As a result of unprecedented population growth and increasing acceptance of female participation in the work force, the number of people seeking jobs in the Middle East and North Africa, a region already plagued by double-digit unemployment rates, will double in the next 50 years. In Algeria, where unemployment stands at 22 percent, the labor force is growing at a staggering 4.2 percent annually, and the number seeking work will more than double by 2050. Egypt alone will need to create 26 million more jobs by 2050 as its total population hits 115 million.[59]

Nations throughout Asia will also see phenomenal increases in the numbers seeking work, including Pakistan, where the work force will grow from 70 million in 1998 to

205 million by 2050. Over the next 25 years, India will add nearly 10 million to its work force each year. During the same period, China will add nearly 6 million annually due to population growth alone, compounding the work shortages caused by the current flood of migrants to China's coastal cities and by massive layoffs—estimated at more than 30 million—as state-run operations are scaled back.[60]

Nations are hard-pressed to educate and train rapidly growing numbers of young people in marketable skills for the global workplace. Moreover, meeting the basic needs of a growing population draws scarce foreign exchange and other resources from investments in education and job creation. Throughout the world, young people entering the work force are increasingly faced with unemployment and social marginalization. In most societies, unemployment rates for those under 25 are substantially higher than for older people.[61]

Surplus farmland once served as a traditional source of employment for growing populations, as new land could be plowed to generate work and income. However, global per capita grainland has dropped by half—and considerably more in certain nations—since 1950. Moreover, the mechanization of agriculture fuels the exodus of job seekers into the world's urban areas, where unemployment is often most acute. Heavily reliant on natural capital in the past, future job creation will require massive amounts of financial capital to jumpstart the industrial and service sectors.[62]

As the balance between the demand and supply of labor is tipped by population growth, wages—the price of labor—tend to decrease. And in a situation of labor surplus, the quality of jobs may not improve as fast, for workers will settle for longer hours, fewer benefits, and less control over work activities.[63]

Employment is the key to obtaining food, housing, health services, and education, in addition to providing self-respect and self-fulfillment. Rising numbers of unemployed people could drive global poverty and hunger to precarious levels, fueling political instability.[64]

Cropland

Since mid-century, global population has grown much faster than the cropland area. The trend is likely to continue in the next century, dropping cropland per person to historically low levels. The ever smaller per capita cropland base will make food self-sufficiency impossible for many countries, and will test the capacity of international markets to meet a growing demand for imported food.[65]

For millennia, farmers satisfied rising food demand by bringing new land under the plow. But by mid-century cropland expansion could no longer meet the food needs of an increasingly populous and prosperous world. The 10,000-year era of steady expansion was over, and a new era began that stressed raising land productivity. As this high-yielding era shows signs of faltering, concern over the shrinking supply of cropland per person looms ever larger.[66]

Since mid-century, grain area—which serves as a proxy for cropland in general—has increased by some 19 percent, but global population has grown 132 percent, seven times faster. Largely as a result, grain area per person has fallen by half since 1950, from 0.24 to 0.12 hectares—about one sixth the size of a soccer field. (See Figure 6.) Assuming that grain area remains constant, grain area per person will fall to 0.07 hectares by 2050. In crowded industrial countries such as Japan, Taiwan, and South Korea, grain area per capita today is smaller than the area of a tennis court.[67]

As grain area per person falls, more and more nations risk losing the capacity to feed themselves. The trend is illustrated starkly in the world's four fastest-growing large countries. Having already seen per capita grain area shrink by 40–50 percent between 1960 and 1998, Pakistan, Nigeria, Ethiopia, and Iran can expect a further 60–70 percent loss by 2050—a conservative projection that assumes no further losses of agricultural land. The result will be four countries with a combined population of more than 1 billion whose grain area per person will be only 300–600 square meters,

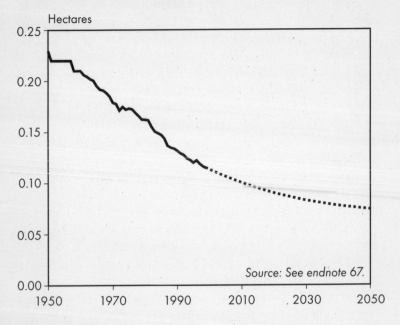

FIGURE 6

World Grain Harvested Area Per Person, 1950–98, with Projections to 2050

Source: See endnote 67.

less than a quarter of the area in 1950.[68]

The historical record suggests that such a small area per person will send a substantial share of a country's people to world markets for their food. Consider the experience of six countries in East Asia whose per capita grain area currently ranges from 200 to 600 square meters per person. Sri Lanka relies on imports for more than a third of its grain, while Japan, Taiwan, South Korea, and Malaysia buy more than 70 percent of their grain from abroad. North Korea is the only one of the six that does not import heavily (it gets less than 20 percent of its grain requirements from abroad), but its population is poorly fed—indeed, on the verge of starvation.[69]

The concern is that population growth will push many nations—not just the four fastest-growing ones—below the 600-square meter-threshold in coming decades. In Asia alone, where grain area per person stands at 800 square meters, 16 countries are poised to cross this threshold by 2050, and many of them much sooner. As this process unfolds, the number of people who will turn to foreign markets for their food will likely jump sharply. These countries will find an increasingly tight international grain market, with nations from the Middle East, North Africa, and other regions already buying a third or more of their grain overseas.[70]

In addition to per capita losses, population growth can lead to degradation of cropland, reducing its productivity or even eliminating it from production. As a country's population density increases and good farmland becomes scarce, poor farmers are forced onto ecologically vulnerable land such as hillsides and tropical forest. In the Philippines, for example, hillside agriculture accounted for only 10 percent of all agricultural land in 1960, but 30 percent in 1987. Because it is highly erodible, hillside land is easily damaged; worldwide, some 160 million hectares of hillside farmland—11 percent of cropland—were characterized in 1989 as "severely eroded." Similarly, population pressure can force peasants to overfarm the poor soils of tropical forests. After being cleared and farmed for a few years, these soils typically require fallow periods of 20–25 years, but population pressures keep poor farmers on the same land for far longer than the soil can support, cutting fallow periods to just a few years in some areas of tropical Africa and Asia.[71]

Finally, population pressures on a fixed base of land can result in rural landlessness. In Bangladesh, for example, landlessness among rural households rose from 35 percent in 1960 to 53 percent in the early 1990s. Interestingly, Bangladesh is regarded as a success in slowing population expansion, as its growth rate declined from 2.8 percent in the late 1970s to 1.5 percent in the early 1990s. But its success came too late to prevent the increase in rural landlessness, highlighting the need to work sooner, rather than later, for population stabilization.[72]

Forests

Global losses of forest area have marched in step with population growth for much of human history. The two trends rose slowly for millennia, turned upward in recent centuries, and accelerated sharply after 1900. Indeed, 75 percent of the historical growth in global population and an estimated 75 percent of the loss in global forested area have occurred in the twentieth century. The correlation makes sense, given the additional need for farmland, pastureland, and forest products as human numbers expand. But since 1950, the advent of mass consumption of forest products has quickened the pace of deforestation. (See Table 6.)[73]

In some cases, population pressure is still closely linked with deforestation. In Latin America, for example, ranching is the single largest cause of deforestation. Because most meat produced in Latin America is consumed there, and because meat consumption per person has been largely unchanged for several decades, it is likely that expanding population is the principal reason for ranching-related deforestation. In addition, analysts at the World Resources Institute estimate that overgrazing and overcollection of firewood—which are often a function of a growing population—are degrading some 14 percent of the world's threatened frontier forests (large areas of virgin forest). In fact, a U.N. Food and Agriculture Organization study showed a one-to-one correlation between population growth and fuelwood consumption in 16 Asian countries between 1961 and 1994.[74]

On the other hand, deforestation created by the demand for forest products tracks more closely with rising per capita consumption in recent decades. Global use of paper and paperboard per person, for example, has doubled (or nearly tripled) since 1961, and most of the increase has come in wealthy countries with low or even stable levels of population growth. Europe, Japan, and North America, with 16 percent of global population, consume 63 percent of the world's

TABLE 6

Forested Area Per Capita, 1995, with Projections to 2050

Region	Forested Area Per Capita	
	1995	2050
	(hectares)	
Africa	0.32	0.11
Asia	0.12	0.08
Europe and Russia	1.1	1.28
North and Central America	2.07	1.54
Oceania	3.32	2.02
South America	2.14	1.30
World	0.59	0.36

Source: See endnote 73.

paper and paperboard and nearly half its industrial wood.[75]

Although consumption and population growth have operated somewhat independently in the late twentieth century, the two forces could coincide in the developing world in coming decades, with substantial consequences for forests. Developing-country paper consumption is less than one tenth the level found in industrial nations, suggesting that large increases in consumption are likely as these nations prosper. (It also suggests that greater economy is needed in industrial countries.) With 80 percent of the world's people, and as home to all of the increase in population in coming decades, even modest growth in per capita paper and wood consumption in developing countries could place substantial pressure on forests. If paper were used by the entire world in 2050 at today's industrial-nation rates, paper production would need to jump more than eightfold over 1996 levels.[76]

This projected growth is unsustainable, given that global use of forest products is already near or beyond the limits of sustainable use. Using data on sustainable forest yields, and assuming that virgin forests are left intact, researchers at Friends of the Earth UK have determined that production of forest products for the world is 25 percent beyond the most restrictive estimates for sustainable consumption. (Many forests, of course, are already logged well beyond sustainable levels.) The most optimistic assessment would allow for a further 35-percent growth in consumption. Even that spells trouble, however, given a projected global population increase of some 54 percent over the next half-century, and given the likely increase in consumption from rising prosperity. Lower consumption of forest products and increased recycling in industrial countries can make room for a more prosperous developing world to enjoy the products of the world's forests, but the task will be made easier if population growth everywhere is stabilized sooner rather than later.[77]

If population and consumption eat into the world's forests, the resulting loss of forest services reduces, in turn, a country's capacity to support its population. Forests provide habitat to a diverse selection of wildlife; tropical forests, for example, are home to more than 50 percent of the world's species. And as storehouses of carbon, forests are key to regulating climate. Deforestation leads to huge releases of carbon: an estimated one quarter of the world's carbon emissions come from forest clearing. Loss of these macroservices undermines the stability and resiliency of the global environment on which economies—and populations—depend. In addition, forests provide services vital to a local population, such as control of erosion, steady provision of water across rainy and dry seasons, and regulation of rainfall. Taken together, the loss of these services due to deforestation can upset local economies and subject local populations to economic instability.[78]

Housing

Over the past half-century, the world's housing stock has grown roughly in step with population. Yet for more and more people worldwide, adequate and affordable housing remains beyond reach, driving some into substandard dwellings and slums and others onto the street. This situation stands to worsen, for the need for housing worldwide is projected to nearly double over the next 50 years.[79]

Although industrial nations currently occupy a disproportionately large share of the world's households relative to their population, virtually all future growth will occur in developing countries, where housing requirements will more than double by the middle of the twenty-first century. (See Table 7.) This phenomenal growth results from the potent synergy between population growth and a shift toward fewer people per household—a trend that is especially pronounced where economic growth is rapid.[80]

HABITAT, the United Nations Centre for Human Settlements, has projected housing requirements based on roughly a 30-percent reduction in people per household over the next 50 years. These figures are purely statistical estimates and do not consider possible checks in housing growth, such as materials or financial constraints, intensified land competition, or increased poverty. Our own projections assume that household size will indeed decrease, as fertility rates drop and as extended families become more rare, but by a more modest 15 percent.

Over the next 50 years, housing needs in Africa and the Middle East are expected to increase more than threefold, with tremendous gains in the region's most populous nations; demands are to increase 3.5 times in Nigeria and 4.5 times in Ethiopia. Although less dramatic percentage increases are expected in Asia, the doubling of households in the region will require nearly 700 million additional homes by 2050. Still, some countries there, such as Pakistan and neighboring Afghanistan, will see housing needs increase

TABLE 7

Number of Households Worldwide, 1995, with Projections to 2050

	1995	2050	Additional Housing Required	Change, 1995-2050
	(million)			(percent)
World	1,403	2,573	1,170	83
Industrial Nations	439	513	73	17
Developing Nations	964	2,061	1,097	114

Source: See endnote 80.

nearly three and a half times.[81]

The projected growth in housing needs becomes all the more daunting given that rapid population growth—combined with rapid urban growth—has already left a large share of the world's population without adequate housing. HABITAT estimates that at least 600 million urban dwellers and more than 1 billion rural dwellers in Africa, Asia, and Latin America live in housing that is "so overcrowded and of such poor quality with such inadequate provision for water, sanitation, drainage, and garbage collection that their lives and their health are continually at risk."[82]

As the supply of housing falls behind demand, the quality of available housing tends to deteriorate. Cheaper, less durable materials, such as scrap metal and cardboard, are substituted for more expensive, weather-resistant materials, such as concrete and wood. Fierce competition in swelling urban areas for desirable land can eliminate all hope of low-income households acquiring a plot for housing. As choice of location dwindles, shantytowns and other low-quality settlements develop on marginal land ill suited for housing—in floodplains, on steep hillsides, near garbage dumps or other environmentally risky sites. From New York to Beijing, cities are faced with land and materials constraints even as their populations continue to grow.[83]

At the same time, housing area per person continues to increase in certain nations and among the more affluent segments of other nations, placing additional stress on prime space and building materials. In the United States, Western Europe, and Japan—a nation traditionally known for small dwellings—floor space per person has more than doubled in new single family homes since mid-century. The global disparity in floor space per person—Washington, D.C., at the high end with 70 square meters per person, and most of humanity at around 9 square meters per person—will likely mimic the growing global disparity in income, as wealthy households scale up and poorer households fill up.[84]

Housing can provide a connection to a supply of fresh water and sanitation facilities. But as its quality deteriorates, so do these basic amenities. Half the world's people are without access to sanitation and nearly this many—2.7 billion— are without a reliable source of safe drinking water. Shortages of housing that provides these basic services are most acute in cities, where rapid urbanization and high population densities place heightened demands on infrastructure. And still housing needs are projected to soar in the regions of the world where access to water and sanitation are most constrained.[85]

The ultimate manifestation of population growth outstripping the supply of housing is homelessness. The United Nations estimates that at least 100 million of the world's people—roughly the same as the population of Mexico— have no home; the number tops 1 billion if those with especially insecure or temporary accommodations, such as squatters, are included. In many developing countries, squatter communities are home to 30–60 percent of the urban population. There are some 250,000 pavement dwellers in Bombay alone. In Latin America, *los niños de las calles* (children of the streets)—humans who are born, live, and die in the streets—are common in all major cities. Unless the world moves to a lower population trajectory, the ranks of homeless are likely to swell dramatically.[86]

Energy

It has been scarcely 200 years—the dawn of the Industrial Revolution—since humans abandoned sole reliance on firewood, other biomass fuels, and direct sunlight to meet daily energy needs. In the past half-century, global demand for energy grew twice as fast as population, as industrial nations burned coal, oil, and natural gas to fuel their economies. (See Figure 7.) Over the next half-century, world energy demands are projected to continue expanding beyond population growth, as developing countries try to catch up with industrial nations.[87]

Developing countries will see tremendous growth in energy consumption in the next half-century, as growing populations and increasing affluence combine to drive their energy demands to dizzying levels. Based on projections from the U.S. Department of Energy and the Intergovernmental Panel on Climate Change, total energy consumption in the developing world will grow by 336 percent—nearly three times faster than population—over the next 50 years, from 3,499 million tons of oil equivalent to 15,255 million tons. By 2030, energy consumption in the developing world will likely surpass usage in industrial nations.

Rising per capita consumption accounts for nearly two thirds of the growth in energy demand in poorer nations, but different population trajectories can have dramatic effects on future demands. For example, assuming the same growth in per capita energy demand, moving to the low U.N. population projection will reduce total energy demands from developing countries by 2,792 million tons of oil equivalent—the output of nearly 3,000 average-sized coal-fired power plants.

In the next 50 years, the greatest growth in energy demands will come where economic activity is projected to be highest: in Asia, where consumption is expected to grow 361 percent, though population will grow by just 50 percent. Energy consumption in Latin America and Africa is project-

FIGURE 7

Global Energy Use Per Person, 1950–95, with Projections to 2050

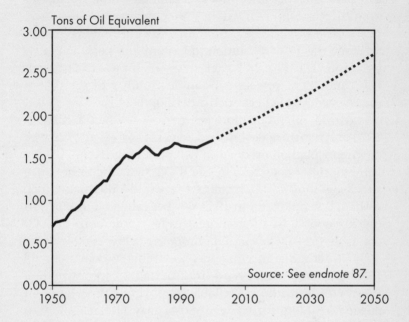

Source: See endnote 87.

ed to increase by 340 percent and 326 percent, respectively. Lower rates of population growth in Asia, compared with Latin America and Africa, mean that energy use per person will increase most in Asia. Nonetheless, in all three regions, local pressures on energy sources, ranging from forests to fossil fuel reserves to waterways, will be significant.

When per capita energy consumption is high, even a low rate of population growth can have significant effects on total energy demand. In the United States, for example, where current per capita energy demand is nearly double that in other industrial nations and over 13 times that in developing countries, the 75 million people projected to be added in the next 50 years will boost energy demands by 758 million tons of oil equivalent—roughly the same as the present energy consumption of Africa and Latin America.

World energy use per person doubled between 1950 and 1973, before confronting a short-term slowdown when restricted exports from oil-producing nations drove up energy prices. Another price shock, combined with a global economic recession, resulted in the slowdown of the early 1980s. The most recent stumbling block in energy growth followed the 1989 revolution in Eastern Europe, when energy use in the former Soviet states plummeted. Although DOE and IPCC project substantial future growth, similar forces may act to check such a development.

World oil production per person reached a high in 1979 and has since declined 23 percent. Moreover, estimates of when global oil production will peak range from 2011 by Petroconsultants to 2025 by the IPCC, signaling future price shocks as long as oil remains the world's dominant fuel. Although people born in 1950 saw per capita oil production quickly double in a few short decades, those born in 2000 are likely to see it cut in half, dropping below 1950 levels.[88]

In addition, meeting increased energy demands will require more storage and transportation infrastructure. Communities without a reliable supply of clean water or an adequate system for waste disposal may also fall short in connection to power supplies. For the estimated 2 billion who are still off the grid—and also experiencing high rates of population growth—decentralized energy technologies, such as solar roof shingles and fuel cell power generators, are likely the most feasible and affordable option for meeting increased energy demands.[89]

Yet it will not necessarily be the scarcity of fuel that constrains future growth in energy consumption, but rather concerns about climate change, air quality, and water quality. Growing climate concerns will require massive reductions in fossil fuel use at a time when demand for energy is soaring. A shift to renewable energy sources, such as solar energy and wind power, in addition to continued efficiency gains for power plants, cars, and appliances, holds great promise for meeting future energy demands without adverse ecological consequences.

Urbanization

The world's cities are growing far faster than its population. Indeed, aside from the growth of population itself, urbanization is the dominant demographic trend of the half-century now ending. In 1950, 750 million of the world's people lived in cities. By 1996, this had at least tripled, to more than 2.6 billion. The number projected to live in cities by 2050, some 6.5 billion people, exceeds world population today. (See Table 8.)[90]

Urbanization on anything like the scale that we know today is historically quite recent. In 1800, only one city—London—had a million people. Today, 326 cities have at least that many people. And there are 14 megacities, those with 10 million or more residents. Tokyo is the largest, at 27 million. Mexico City is second, at 17 million. New York City and São Paulo are close behind, with 16 million each. Rounding out the list in descending size are Bombay (15 million), Shanghai (14), Los Angeles (12), Calcutta (12), Buenos Aires (12), Seoul (12), Beijing (11), Osaka (11), Lagos (10), Rio de Janeiro (10), and Delhi (10).[91]

The rate of growth of cities in industrial countries during the first century or so of the Industrial Revolution was relatively slow. Today's cities are growing much faster. It took London 130 years to get from 1 million to 8 million. Mexico City made this jump in just 30 years.[92]

Measured in annual growth, some cities, such as Lagos, Nigeria, are growing at 5 percent a year; Bombay is growing at nearly 4 percent. The world's urban population as a whole is growing by just over 1 million people each week. This urban growth is fed by the natural increase of urban populations, by net migration from the countryside, and by villages or towns expanding to the point where they become cities or they are absorbed by the spread of existing cities.[93]

During the early stages of industrialization, urbanization was largely in response to the pull of employment opportunities in cities. More recently, however, the move-

TABLE 8

World Population and Urbanization, 1950–90, with Projections to 2050*

Year	Population	Urban Population	Urban Share of Total
	(billion)		(percent)
1950	2.5	0.8	30
1960	3.0	1.0	34
1970	3.7	1.4	36
1980	4.4	1.8	39
1990	5.3	2.3	43
2000	6.1	2.9	47
2010	6.9	3.6	52
2020	7.7	4.4	57
2030	8.4	5.1	61
2040	8.9	5.8	65
2050	9.4	6.5	69

*U.N. projections only go to 2030; figures for 2040 and 2050 are Worldwatch extrapolations.
Source: See endnote 90.

ment from countryside to city has been more the result of rural push than of urban pull. It is a reflection of the lack of opportunity in the countryside as already small plots of land are divided and then divided again with each passing generation, until they become so small that people can no longer make a living from them.

Historically, cities and the surrounding countryside had a symbiotic relationship, with the latter supplying food and raw materials in exchange for manufactured products. Today cities are tied much more to each other and to the global economy. The food and fuel that once came from the surrounding countryside now often comes from distant corners of the planet.

As societies urbanize, the use of basic resources, such as energy and water, rises. In traditional rural societies, for example, people live on the land and thus do not need to travel to work. But once they migrate to cities, commuting becomes the rule, not the exception. In villages, most of the food that is consumed is produced locally, requiring little energy for processing, packaging, and transportation; once people move into cities, on the other hand, virtually all their food must be brought in. In a village where residents typically draw their water from a central well and carry it to their homes, water use is necessarily limited. But when villagers move to urban high-rise apartment buildings with indoor plumbing, replete with showers and flush toilets, water consumption soars.

The ecology of cities is a continuing challenge to city managers simply because cities require the concentration of huge quantities of water, food, energy, and raw materials. The waste products must then be dispersed or the city will become uninhabitable. As cities become larger, the disposal of residential and industrial wastes becomes ever more challenging.

Partly as a result of the mounting pressure for people to migrate to cities, the growth in urban populations is far outstripping the availability of basic services, such as water, sewerage, transportation, and electricity. As a result, life in urban shantytowns is plagued by poverty, pollution, congestion, homelessness, and unemployment.[94]

Since the beginning of the Industrial Revolution, the terms of trade between countryside and city have favored the latter simply because cities control the scarce resources in development, namely capital and technology. But if the price of food rises in the years ahead, as now seems likely, the terms of trade could shift, favoring the countryside. If in the new world of the twenty-first century the scarce resources are land and water, those controlling them could have the upper hand in determining rural/urban terms of trade.

This aside, if recent trends continue, within the next several years more than half of us will be living in cities—making the world more urban than rural for the first time in history. We will have become an urban species, far removed from our hunter-gatherer origins.

Natural Recreation Areas

Population growth during the past 50 years has made it difficult to set aside and conserve natural areas. Another half-century of growth will put even more pressure on protected areas as formerly small, distant settlements encroach on these sites and as the number of people (both local and visitors) who use these sites explodes.[95]

National parks, forests, wildlife preserves, beaches, and other protected areas offer sanctuary to various habitats and indigenous communities, in addition to providing resources for local peoples. In an urbanizing world, these sites provide an opportunity for healthy interaction with the natural environment, as well as rare serenity.

From Buenos Aires to Bangkok, dramatic population growth in the world's major cities—and the sprawl and pollution they bring—threatens natural recreation areas that lay beyond city limits. Tremendous growth in the population of Bombay has already engulfed Borivili National Park, a reserve that was beyond the city's periphery only a decade ago. With projected growth of 60 percent in the next 20 years, Bombay may soon swallow up more distant areas. On every continent, human encroachment has reduced both the size and the quality of natural recreation areas. (See Table 9.)[96]

In nations where rapid population growth has outstripped the carrying capacity of local resources, protected areas become especially vulnerable. Although in industrial nations these areas are synonymous with camping, hiking, and picnics in the country, in Asia, Africa, and Latin America most national parks, forests, and preserves are inhabited or used for natural resources by local populations.[97]

An assessment by the World Conservation Union– IUCN of 30 protected sites in the developing world shows that these areas now act as magnets, attracting people to the rich oasis of water, fuel, food, and other resources they contain. Population growth rates in and around these areas are typically 2 percentage points above the national average—largely

TABLE 9

Primary Threats and Conservation Issues, Selected Protected Areas

Protected Area and Country	Primary Threats and Conservation Issues
Lake Nakuru catchment basin, Kenya	High rates of in-migration contribute to land fragmentation and deforestation around the lake; intensive subsistence farming leads to soil erosion; industrial and domestic effluent from growing Nakuru town; increased tourism.
Jaldapara Wildlife Sanctuary, West Bengal, India	Villagers around the sanctuary are heavily dependent on its resources; villager population doubled from 1971 to 1991 and continues to grow; 25 percent of households are landless and they derive 90 percent of their income from the sanctuary (from sale of firewood, cotton floss, and grass); in-migration is also high.
Everglades National Park, Florida, United States	Population growth (combined populations of Miami and Fort Lauderdale have grown sevenfold since 1950), soaring water demands, and drainage of wetlands for housing, golf courses, and agricultural expansion threaten the park's health while shrinking its borders.
Royal Bardia National Park, Terai region, Nepal	Population growth (at 3.5 percent annually, with a total fertility rate of 6.6 children per woman), in-migration, and tourism contribute to shortages of fuelwood, fodder for livestock, and small timber for construction; this encourages locals to use park resources to meet needs, visitors to the Himalayas have grown from a few hundred in 1970 to 90,000 a year today.

Source: See endnote 96.

as a result of immigration from resource-starved areas.[98]

As people seek out scarce resources, the resulting concentrations can be devastating. For example, population densities in the region surrounding Bwindi Impenetrable National Park in southern Uganda are some of the highest in all of Africa—exceeding 250 people per square kilometer. Though population at this site is expected to multiply, chronic land hunger already precipitates conflicts over fuel-wood collection, farming, cattle grazing, and bush burning.[99]

Migration-driven population growth also endangers natural recreation areas in many industrial nations. Everglades National Park faces collapse as millions of new-comers move into South Florida.[100]

Coastal recreation areas, including beaches, may be most burdened by the formidable combination of popula-tion growth and migration. All but one of the world's 15 largest cities—Mexico City—are coastal, and all of these cities will grow in the decades ahead. Whether it takes the form of expanding shantytowns in Kingston, Jamaica, or sprawling tract housing in southern California, virtually all the growth and movement in population in the next 50 years will occur in densely populated coastal corridors.[101]

In nations already struggling to meet basic human needs, the prospect of establishing additional protected areas becomes increasingly slim. Throughout India, for example, while the national government designates areas as protected, state and local governments work to de-reserve these sites so that the resources can be harnessed to meet the needs of an additional 18 million Indians each year.[102]

Sunbathers on beaches in Japan are often compared to sardines. People who use Central Park in New York City, which has nearly doubled in population since 1950, are faced with growing congestion and restrictions on activities. National parks throughout North America are confronted with huge backlogs of requests to visit, having to turn tourists away. Tourism at Yosemite has boomed from rough-ly 4,000 visitors in 1886 to more than 4 million people (and their cars) today. It is often remarked that "Americans love their national parks to death," as increased visitation degrades campsites, trails, and wilderness.[103]

Longer waiting lists and higher user fees for fewer secluded spots are likely the tip of the iceberg, as population growth threatens to eliminate the diversity of habitats and cultures, in addition to the peace and quiet, that protected areas currently house.

Education

In contrast to the food supply challenge posed by the coming wave of population growth, the global need for teachers and classrooms will rise very slowly in the next half-century. In many countries, the school-age population is increasing much less rapidly than the overall national population. The trend illustrates that growth rates typically differ for different age strata of the population. It also shows that declining birth rates can take decades to move through an entire population.

At the global level, for example, total population is projected to increase by 54 percent between 2000 and 2050, but the number of children aged 5 to 14 will grow by only 6 percent. (See Figure 8.) And 14 of the world's largest countries—accounting for 60 percent of global population in

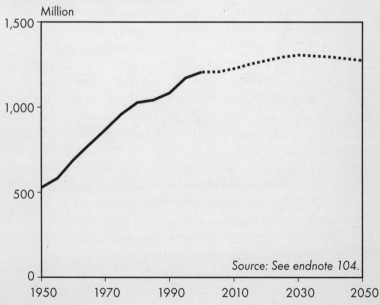

FIGURE 8

World Population of Children Aged 5 to 14, 1950–95, with Projections to 2050

Source: See endnote 104.

TABLE 10

Children Aged 5 to 14, Selected Countries, 1995 and 2050

Country	School-age Population		Change in School-age Population,	
	1995	2050	1995	2050
	(million)		(percent)	
China	217	190	-27	-12
India	213	198	-16	- 7
United States	39	43	+ 4	+10
Indonesia	43	42	- 1	- 2
Brazil	35	32	- 3	- 8
Russia	23	12	- 9	-39
Pakistan	35	53	+18	+51
Japan	14	11	- 3	-21
Bangladesh	36	30	- 6	- 17
Nigeria	30	53	+23	+77

Source: See endnote 104.

1995—will actually begin to see decreases in the number of children aged 5 to 14 by 2015; for several of these countries, the decline in this age group has already begun. (See Table 10.) These countries will need fewer classrooms and teachers to educate the youngest members of society (assuming they maintain current class size and student-teacher ratios).[104]

Plenty of nations, however, still have increasing child-age populations. Where countries have not acted to stabilize population, the base of the national population pyramid continues to expand, and pressures on the educational system will be severe. In the world's 10 fastest-growing countries, for example, most of which are in Africa and the Middle East, the child-age population will increase an average 93 percent over the next half-century. Africa as a whole will see its school-age population grow by 75 percent through 2040.

The rapid growth in African populations is especially worrisome because of the extra burden it imposes in a region already lagging in education. Only 56 percent of Africans south of the Sahara are literate, compared with 71 percent for all developing countries. Few African countries have universal primary education, and secondary education reaches only 4–5 percent of African children. Educating today's children is challenge enough; the addition of another three students for every four already there will require heroic investments in education. But the alternative is grim: without additional investment in education, today's average student-teacher ratio of 42 in sub-Saharan Africa will reach 75 by 2040.[105]

Many countries will be challenged to increase funding for education while ensuring that other worthy sectors also receive the support they need. With 900 million illiterate adults in the world, the case for a renewed commitment to education is easy to make. But competing for these funds are the 840 million chronically hungry and the 1.2 billion without access to a decent toilet.

The budget stresses on governments attempting to meet these basic needs would clearly be reduced with smaller populations. Mozambique and Lesotho, for example, both met the UNESCO benchmark for investment in education in 1992—6 percent of gross domestic product—and the two countries' economies were roughly equal in size. Yet because Mozambique has many times the population of Lesotho, spending per child in Lesotho is about nine times higher than in Mozambique. For the majority of countries who do not meet the UNESCO funding standard, many of whom also fall short in providing other basic services, a decline in population pressure could help substantially to meet all of their social goals.[106]

If national education systems begin to stress life-long learning for a rapidly changing world, as recommended by a 1998 UNESCO report on education in the twenty-first century, then extensive provision for adult education will be necessary, affecting even those countries with shrinking child-age populations. Such a development means that countries that started population stabilization programs earliest will be in the best position to educate their entire citizenry.

Waste

A growing population increases society's disposal headaches—the garbage, sewage, and industrial waste that must be gotten rid of. Even where population is largely stable—the case in many industrial countries—-the flow of waste products into landfills and waterways generally continues to increase. Where high rates of economic and population growth coincide in coming decades, as they will in many developing countries, mountains of waste will likely pose difficult disposal challenges for municipal and national authorities. (See Table 11.)[107]

Data for waste generation in the developing world are scarce, but citizens in many of these countries are estimated to produce roughly half a kilo of municipal waste each day. If this figure is applied to today's population, a total of 824 million tons of municipal waste is being churned out annually in developing countries. Population growth alone would boost this number to 1.5 billion tons by 2050. But waste rates tend to climb with rising incomes; a developing world generating as much waste per capita as industrial countries do today would be producing some 3.6 billion tons of municipal waste in 2050. Moreover, prosperity boosts the volume of waste as the share of plastics, metal, paper, and other nonorganics rises.[108]

Local and global environmental effects of waste disposal will likely worsen as 3.4 billion people are added to global population over the next half-century. Acids from organic wastes, for example, and poisons from hazardous wastes often leach from landfills, polluting local groundwater supplies. And rotting organic matter generates methane, a greenhouse gas. If the waste is incinerated rather than thrown into landfills, cities will have to worry about increases in cancer-causing dioxin emissions, one of the byproducts of burning garbage.

Meanwhile, today's largely unmet sanitation needs could also be greatly exacerbated by population growth.

TABLE 11

Challenges for Waste Management in Developing Countries

Category of Waste	Source of Increased Waste	Disposal Problems
Municipal Solid Waste	Prosperity increases both the weight and volume of waste per person. The average American produces roughly four times as much municipal solid waste as someone in the developing world. Plastic—emblematic of an industrial throwaway society—requires more than six times as much volume per unit of weight as food does.	Unless expensive infrastructure is installed, dumps and landfills leach pollutants into groundwater and pose serious health risks to neighbors. They also generate methane, a greenhouse gas. Incinerators can be a serious source of dioxin emissions. And dumping in oceans or other bodies of water creates serious water pollution problems.
Industrial Waste	Industrial waste also increases rapidly as economies prosper. The International Maritime Organization estimated that developing countries produce roughly 6 kilos of hazardous waste per person, but that Eastern Europe generates 50 kilos, and other industrial nations, 100 kilos.	To avoid the hazardous waste legacy of industrial countries—the U.S. Superfund sites; the toxic dumping of Eastern Europe, Russia, and China—developing nations will need to build special disposal facilities. Yet 45 of 74 countries surveyed by the International Maritime Organization report that hazardous waste is unregulated.
Human and Animal Waste	Human waste grows in step with population, but animal waste may grow more rapidly as prospering countries expand the size of their stocks to meet a growing demand for meat.	Providing adequate sanitation to the unserved half of the world—and for the billions yet to come—can be very expensive. As livestock raising becomes more centralized, managing animal waste requires capital-intensive facilities, in contrast to the simple waste-to-cropland recycling system long used on farms.

Source: See endnote 107.

Half the world's people do not have access to a decent toilet, according to UNESCO and the World Health Organization. Lack of sanitation is a leading cause of disease: WHO reports that half the developing world suffers from one of the six diseases associated with poor water supply and sanitation. One of these, diarrhea, is the biggest killer of children today, taking an estimated 2.2 million young lives each year. Unless the expected growth in population of the developing world is matched by an increased commitment to provide adequate sanitation, these health problems are likely to expand.[109]

While the greatest shortage of sanitation is found in rural areas, the need is most urgent in cities, because of the greater potential there for pathogen-tainted water to sicken people on a massive scale. This urban need poses a particular challenge, because the ranks of city dwellers will swell in the next century. In contrast to global population, which is projected to increase by 54 percent over the next half-century, cities will see much greater growth—about 128 percent. Developing-country cities, which failed to meet the sanitation needs of more than a half-billion residents in 1994, will be hard-pressed to service the more than 3 billion people who will be added to cities in the next 50 years.[110]

Prospects for providing access to sanitation are dismal in the near to medium term. Just to keep from losing ground, the rate of provision of service to urban dwellers needs to more than double in Asia. In Africa, it would have to increase by 33 times. And to achieve full coverage by 2020, service provision would have to triple in Asia and increase by 46 times in Africa. Despite the attention focused on sanitation, governments have not demonstrated the will to meet this growing challenge.[111]

Meat Production

World meat production increased from 44 million tons in 1950 to 211 million tons in 1997, expanding almost twice as fast as population. In per capita terms, world meat production expanded from 17 kilograms in 1950 to 36 kilograms in 1997, more than doubling. (See Figure 9.) Growth in meat production was originally concentrated in western industrial countries and Japan, but over the last two decades it has increased rapidly in East Asia (especially China), the Middle East, and Latin America.[112]

When incomes begin to rise in traditional low-income societies, one of the first things people do is diversify their diets, consuming more livestock products. People everywhere appear to have an innate desire to consume at least moderate quantities of meat, perhaps reflecting our evolutionary history as hunter-gatherers.

Three types of meat—beef, pork, and poultry—account for the bulk of world consumption; mutton ranks a distant fourth. From 1950 until 1980, beef and pork production followed the same trend, but after the economic reforms in China—where pork is dominant—pork production surged ahead, climbing from 45 million tons to nearly 90 million tons in less than two decades.[113]

Historically, growth in the world meat supply came primarily from beef and mutton, sustained by the world's rangelands. These areas, consisting mostly of land that is too arid to support crop production, cover a vast part of the planet, roughly double the cropland area. Not only do the herds of cattle and flocks of sheep and goats provide meat and milk, but for millions of people in Africa, the Middle East, Central Asia, parts of the Indian subcontinent, and western China, they provide a livelihood. The only feasible way that this land can contribute to the world's food supply is to graze cattle, sheep, and goats on it, producing the meat and milk that directly and indirectly sustain a large segment of humanity.

FIGURE 9

World Meat Production Per Person, 1950–97

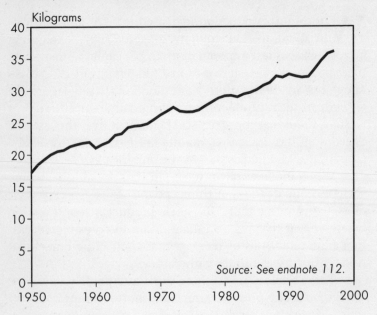

Source: See endnote 112.

In recent years, beef and mutton production have lev-
eled off at just over 60 million tons per year as the number
of animals has pressed against the carrying capacity of rangelands. With little unused grazing capacity left, future gains in
meat production will have to come largely from feeding animals grain. At this point, the relative conversion efficiency
of various animals begins to influence production trends.
Producing a kilogram of beef in the feedlot requires roughly
seven kilograms of grain, while a kilogram of pork requires
nearly four of grain and a kilogram of poultry, just over two.
As grain supplies tighten, the advantage shifts from beef to
pork and even more so to poultry. This helps explain why
world poultry production overtook that of beef in 1996.[114]

Of the world grain harvest of 1.87 billion tons in 1998,
an estimated 37 percent—or nearly 700 million tons—will be
used to feed livestock and poultry, producing milk and eggs as
well as meat. This share, remarkably stable for the last decade,

could go up or down depending on future grain prices.[115]

Expanding world meat production also depends on soybean production. If the grain fed to livestock or poultry is supplemented with a modest amount of soybean meal (the high protein meal that is left after the oil is extracted), its conversion into meat is much more efficient. Largely as a result of this growing demand for livestock products, world soybean production climbed from 17 million tons in 1950 to 152 million tons in 1997, a gain of ninefold.[116]

To project the future demand for meat, we assume that the growth in meat consumption per person will slow over the next half-century, rising by one half instead of doubling, since some countries are nearing the saturation point. This, combined with the projected growth in population, would push total meat consumption from 211 million tons in 1997 to 513 million tons in 2050, a gain of 302 million tons. If we assume an average of 3 kilograms of grain per kilogram of meat produced, this would require more than 900 million tons of additional grain for feed in 2050, an amount equal to half of current world grain consumption. This would greatly intensify the competition between grain consumed directly and that consumed indirectly as animal protein, calling into question whether such gains in meat consumption will ever materialize.[117]

Grain fed to livestock and poultry is now the principal food reserve in the event of a world food emergency. As of 1990, the world had, in effect, three reserves in the global food system: substantial stocks of grain that could be drawn upon in the event of unexpected shortages, a large area of cropland idled under U.S. farm commodity programs, and grain fed to animals. By 1998, world grain stocks had been depleted to one of the lowest levels on record and the cropland that was idled for half a century was returned to production. The only safety net remaining in the event of a major crop failure is the grain fed to livestock and poultry.[118]

Income

Global economic output, the total of all goods and services produced, grew from $5 trillion in 1950 to $29 trillion in 1997, expanding more than twice as fast as population. This increase of nearly sixfold boosted incomes rather substantially for most of humanity. Growth of the world economy from 1990 to 1997 exceeded the growth during the 10,000 years from the beginning of agriculture until 1950.[119]

Economic output per person climbed from just over $1,900 in 1950 to nearly $5,000 in 1997, a gain of 163 percent. (See Figure 10.) Although there is an enormous income gap between industrial and developing countries, the latter's economies are growing far more rapidly. Growth in industrial countries has slowed to scarcely 2 percent a year during the 1990s, compared with nearly 6 percent a year in developing nations.[120]

The fastest-growing region in the world from 1990 to 1997 was Asia, which averaged nearly 8 percent annually. This growth was led by China, whose economy has been increasing at nearly 10 percent a year throughout much of this decade, making it the world's fastest-growing economy. Since 1980, China's economic output has doubled every eight years.

Incomes have risen most rapidly in developing countries where population growth has slowed the most, including, importantly, the countries of East Asia—South Korea, Taiwan, China, Thailand, Indonesia, and Malaysia. Concentrating early on reducing birth rates helped to boost savings to invest in education, health care, and the infrastructure needed by a modern industrial society.

At the other end of the spectrum, African countries—largely ignoring family planning—have been overwhelmed by the sheer numbers of young people who need to be educated and employed. With population growth rates remaining at close to 3 percent or more a year, most of any economic growth that occurred has been absorbed by the

Gross World Product Per Person, 1950–97

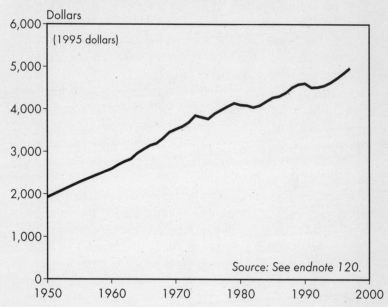

Source: See endnote 120.

increasing population, leaving little to raise incomes.

The enormous growth during the 1990s, particularly in East Asia, is due to the huge increase in private capital flows into developing countries. Between 1990 and 1997, annual private capital flows increased from $42 billion to $256 billion, a gain of more than sixfold. This substantial amount of money dwarfs traditional flows in public funds under international aid programs.[121]

Although incomes in much of the developing world are rising rapidly, they are not rising for everyone. The World Bank estimates that 1.3 billion of the world's people subsist on $1 a day or less. For this one fifth of humanity, trapped at a subhuman level of existence, there has not been any meaningful progress.[122]

The sources of growth are changing. In earlier times, most of the growth was in agriculture. Since the advent of the Industrial Revolution, however, more and more of the growth has been concentrated in industry. Then beginning around mid-century, the services sector—insurance, banking, education—began to expand rapidly, accounting for most of the change in the industrial world. More recently, growth has been concentrated in the information sector as computerization of the economy and telecommunications have grown at extraordinary rates.

The good news is that the global economy has been expanding at a near record pace during the 1990s. The bad news is that the economy, as now structured, is outgrowing the Earth's ecosystem. The result is excessive pressures on the natural systems and resources. As noted in the first section of this paper, from 1950 to 1997 the use of lumber more than doubled. That of paper increased sixfold, the fish catch increased nearly fivefold, grain consumption nearly tripled, fossil fuel burning nearly quadrupled, and air and water pollutants multiplied severalfold. The unfortunate reality is that the economy continues to expand, but the ecosystem on which it depends does not, creating an increasingly stressed relationship.

If the economy were to expand only enough to cover population growth until 2050, it would need to grow from the $29 trillion of 1997 to $47 trillion. This, of course, would merely maintain current incomes, unacceptable though they are for much of humanity. If, on the other hand, the economy were to continue to expand at 3 percent per year, global economic output would reach $138 trillion in the year 2050.

Even the first, more modest, growth projection would likely lead to a deterioration of the Earth's natural systems to the point where the economy itself would begin to decline. It is easy to foresee a scenario of continuing forest destruction, aquifer depletion, and ecosystem collapse that would lead to economic decline. If the world cannot simultaneously convert the economy to one that is environmentally sustainable—one that does not destroy its own support systems—and move to a lower population trajectory, economic decline will be hard to avoid.

Conclusion: Breaking Out or Breaking Down

As noted in the Introduction, the demographic prospect for individual countries has never varied more widely than it does today. In some nations, populations are projected to decline somewhat over the next half-century, while in others they are projected to more than triple. But are such increases realistic? The preceding analysis of 16 dimensions of the population problem raises doubts as to whether the expected population doublings and triplings in scores of developing countries will, in fact, materialize.

To help assess the likelihood that the increases projected by the United Nations will actually occur, we turn to the concept of the demographic transition, formulated by Princeton demographer Frank Notestein in 1945. Among other things, its three stages help explain widely disparate population growth rates. In the first of the three stages, the one prevailing in preindustrial societies, birth rates and death rates are both high, essentially offsetting each other and leading to little or no population growth. As countries begin to modernize, however, death rates fall and countries enter stage two, where death rates are low while birth rates remain high. At this point, population growth typically reaches 3 percent a year—a rate that if sustained leads to a 20-fold increase in a century. Countries cannot long remain in this stage.[123]

As modernization continues, birth rates fall and countries enter the third and final stage of the demographic transition, when birth rates and death rates again balance, but at low levels. At this point, population size stabilizes. Countries rarely ever have exactly zero growth, but here we consider any country with annual growth below 0.4 percent to have an essentially stable population. Among the earliest nations to reach stage three were East Germany, West Germany, Hungary, and Sweden, which achieved stability during the 1970s.

All countries today are in either stage two or stage three. As noted in the Introduction, some 32 industrial countries have made it to stage three, stabilizing their population size. (See Table 12.) The other 150 or so countries, including most of those in Asia, Africa, and Latin America, are in stage two. Within this group 39 countries, those that have seen their fertility fall to replacement level or below, are approaching stage three. These include China and the United States, which are each growing by roughly 1 percent a year.[124]

In mature industrial countries with stable populations, agricultural claims on the Earth's ecosystem are beginning to level off. In the European Union (EU), for example, population has stabilized at roughly 380 million. With incomes already high, grain consumption per person has plateaued at

TABLE 12

Sixteen Countries with Zero Population Growth, 1998

Country	Annual Rate of Natural Increase (percent)	Midyear Population (million)
Belarus	−0.4	10.2
Belgium	+0.1	10.2
Czech Republic	−0.2	10.3
France	+0.3	58.8
Germany	−0.1	82.3
Greece	0	10.5
Hungary	−0.4	10.1
Italy	0	57.7
Japan	+0.2	126.4
Netherlands	+0.3	15.7
Poland	+0.1	38.7
Romania	−0.2	22.5
Russia	−0.5	146.9
Spain	0	39.4
Ukraine	−0.6	50.3
United Kingdom	+0.2	59.1

Source: See endnote 124.

around 470 kilograms a year. As a result, EU member countries, now consuming roughly 180 million tons of grain annually, have essentially stabilized their claims on the Earth's agricultural resources—the first region in the world to do so. (See Figure 11.) And, perhaps more important, since the region is a net exporter of grain, Europe has done this within the limits of its own land and water resources. Likewise, future demand for grain in both North America and Eastern Europe is also projected to remain within the carrying capacity of regional land and water resources.[125]

Not all countries are so fortunate. Over the next half-century, India's population is projected to overtake that of China, as it expands by nearly 600 million people, compared with just under 300 million for China. Whether India—already facing acute shortages of water—can avoid a breakdown of social systems in the face of such an increase

FIGURE 11

Grain Production and Consumption in the European Union, 1960–98

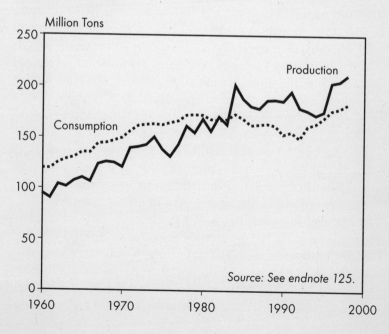

Source: See endnote 125.

in population pressure remains to be seen.

Although there are dozens of countries that now face a doubling or tripling of population size over the next half-century, three of the more populous ones stand out: Ethiopia, Nigeria, and Pakistan. (See Table 13.) The current fertility rate in these countries ranges from just under six children per woman in Pakistan to nearly seven in Ethiopia. By 2050, water availability per person in each of these countries will be well below the minimum needed to satisfy basic food and residential needs.[126]

In addition, there are many smaller countries that are facing potentially overwhelming population growth. Among them are the Congo, going from 49 million today to 165 million in 2050; Yemen, going from 17 million to 89 million; and Tanzania, going from 32 million to 89 million. The latter two are already facing crippling water shortages.

The question now facing the world is whether the 150 or so countries that are still in stage two, with continuing population growth, can make it into stage three by quickly reducing births. Over the next half-century, most countries where population growth is still rapid seem likely to break out of stage two, achieving the demographic stability of stage three. In these nations, the combination of falling fertility, increasing incomes, and rising educational levels will lead to population stabilization within the foreseeable future. Economic and social gains and the decline in fertility will reinforce each other. This can be seen most clearly in the developing countries of East Asia, such as South Korea and Taiwan, where successful early efforts to reduce fertility set the stage for the diversion of capital from rearing large numbers of children to investment in modernization overall. The resulting improvements in living standards then reinforced the trend to smaller families.

Countries that are already pressing against the limits of land and water resources and that are faced with a projected doubling or tripling of their population may face falling living standards that will further reinforce the prevailing high fertility. This reinforcing mechanism, referred to by demog-

TABLE 13

Population in Selected Industrial and Developing Countries in 1998, with Projections to 2050

Area	Population 1998	Population 2050	Increase From 1998 to 2050 (million)	Increase From 1998 to 2050 (percent)
	(million)		(million)	(percent)
Industrial Countries				
United States	274	348	+74	+27
Russia	147	114	-33	-22
Japan	126	110	-16	-13
Germany	82	70	-12	-15
France	59	58	- 1	- 2
United Kingdom	58	59	+ 1	+ 2
Italy	57	42	-15	-26
Developing Countries				
India	976	1,533	+557	+ 57
China	1,255	1,517	+262	+ 21
Pakistan	148	357	+209	+141
Nigeria	122	339	+217	+178
Brazil	165	243	+ 78	+ 47
Bangladesh	124	218	+ 94	+ 76
Ethiopia	62	213	+151	+244
Iran	73	170	+ 97	+133
Congo	49	165	+ 116	+237
Mexico	96	154	+ 58	+ 60
Egypt	66	115	+ 49	+ 74
Tanzania	32	89	+ 57	+178

Source: See endnote 126.

raphers as the demographic trap, could drive countries back into stage one.

Nations in stage two where population is still growing rapidly will thus either shift quickly to smaller families or eventually fall back into stage one of the demographic transition when their economic and social systems break down under mounting population pressure. One or the other of the two self-reinforcing cycles will take over. There are no other options. Among the many countries at risk of falling back into stage one if they do not quickly check their population growth are Afghanistan, Egypt, Ethiopia, Ghana, Haiti, Honduras, India, Myanmar, Nigeria, Pakistan, the Sudan, Tanzania, and Yemen.

Governments of countries that have been in stage two for several decades are typically worn down and drained of financial resources by the consequences of rapid population growth, in effect suffering from demographic fatigue. This includes trying to educate ever growing numbers of children reaching school age, creating jobs for the swelling numbers of young people entering the job market, and dealing with the various environmental problems associated with rapid population growth, such as deforestation, increased flooding and soil erosion, and aquifer depletion. With leadership and fiscal resources stretched thin in trying to cope with so many pressures at once, governments are often unable to respond effectively to emerging threats such as new diseases, water shortages, or food shortages. This is perhaps most evident in the inability of many governments to cope with new diseases, such as AIDS, or the resurgence of more traditional diseases, such as malaria or tuberculosis.

If these threats are not dealt with, they can force countries back into stage one. For several African countries with high HIV infection levels, this is no longer a hypothetical prospect. Although industrial nations have been able to control the spread of the disease, holding infection levels under 1 percent of their populations, governments in many developing countries—already overwhelmed by the pressures just described—have not been able to do so. For example, in Zimbabwe, a country of 11 million people, more than 1.4 million of the adult population of less than 5.6 million are infected with HIV. As a result of this 26-percent adult infection rate and the inability to pay for costly retroviral drugs needed to treat those with the disease, Zimbabwe is expected to reach population stability in the year 2002 as death rates climb to offset birth rates. In effect, it will have fallen back into stage one, marking a tragic new development in world demography.[127]

In contrast to most potentially fatal diseases, AIDS takes its toll not so much among the very young and the elderly, but among the young professionals in the prime of life—the very accountants, engineers, teachers, agronomists, and bankers needed to develop the economy. Again, using Zimbabwe to illustrate, life expectancy—perhaps the best measure of a society's health—is expected to drop from 61 in 1993 to 49 in the year 2000 and, if recent trends continue, to 40 in 2010. Measured by this key social indicator, this represents a reversal of development, turning it back a century or more. These trends are more reminiscent of the Dark Ages than the bright new millennium that many had hoped for.[128]

Other African countries that are also expected to soon reach zero population growth as rising death rates offset high fertility are Botswana (an HIV adult infection rate of 25 percent), Namibia (20 percent), Zambia (19 percent), and Swaziland (18 percent). Other nations where roughly one out of 10 adults is now infected with the virus and where the HIV/AIDS epidemic is spiraling out of control include Burundi, the Central African Republic, the Congo, Côte de Ivoire, Ethiopia, Kenya, Malawi, Mozambique, Rwanda, South Africa, and Tanzania. In the absence of a concerted effort to check the spread of the virus, these countries too are heading for a rise in death rates that will bring their population growth to a halt.[129]

Another situation that could easily become unmanageable is life-threatening shortages of food due to either land or water shortages or both. For example, Pakistan and Nigeria face an impossible challenge in trying to feed their future populations. The projected growth for Pakistan to 357 million by 2050 will reduce its grainland per person from 0.08 hectares at present to 0.03 hectares, roughly the strip between the 10-yard markers on a football field. Nigeria's projected growth will reduce its grainland per person from the currently inadequate 0.15 hectares to 0.05 hectares.[130]

As India's population approaches the 1 billion mark and as it faces the addition of another 600 million people by 2050, it must deal with steep cutbacks in irrigation water.

David Seckler, head of the International Water Management Institute in Sri Lanka, the world's premier water research body, observes in a new study that "the extraction of water from aquifers in India exceeds recharge by a factor of 2 or more. Thus almost everywhere in India, fresh-water aquifers are being pulled down by 1–3 meters per year." Seckler goes on to speculate that as aquifers are depleted, the resulting cutbacks in irrigation could reduce India's harvest by 25 percent. In a country where food supply and demand are precariously balanced and where 18 million people are added to the population each year, the cutbacks in irrigation that are in prospect could drop food supplies below the survival level, creating a national food emergency.[131]

As noted earlier, U.N. demographic projections do not reflect the ecological deterioration and social breakdown of the sort that has led to the ethnic conflicts plaguing countries such as Rwanda and Somalia. Somalia, for example, is still treated by U.N. demographers as a country, but in reality it is not. It is a geographical area inhabited by warring clans—one where ongoing conflict, disintegration of health care services, and widespread hunger combine to raise mortality.

Exactly how the stresses of social disintegration will manifest themselves as the needs of a growing population outstrip the resource base varies from country to country. For example, Rwanda's 1950 population of 2.5 million had reached roughly 8.5 million by early 1994. A country whose agricultural development was once cited as a model for others in Africa saw its grainland area per person shrink to a meager 0.03 hectares per person, less than one third as much as in Bangladesh. In this society, which is almost entirely rural with no industrial cities to migrate to, cropland per person has shrunk to the point where it will no longer adequately feed many of those living on the land, giving rise to a quiet desperation. The resulting tension can easily be ignited—as it was when a long-standing ethnic conflict between Tutsis and Hutus broke out again in 1994, leading to the slaughter of a half-million Rwandans, mostly Tutsis.[132]

The press focused on the long-standing conflict, which

was real, but what was not reported was the extraordinary population growth over the last half-century and how it was affecting the hope of Rwandans for a better future. Desperate people resort to desperate actions.

The issues discussed here raise several complex questions. For example, what is the psychological effect on a society that loses a substantial share of its adult population in a matter of years? What happens when aquifer depletion starts shrinking the food supply in countries with fast-growing populations? Will governments that have permitted AIDS to decimate their populations or that have allowed aquifers to be depleted lose their legitimacy and be voted out or overthrown? No one knows the answer to these questions because continuing rapid population growth and the problems it eventually generates are taking the world into uncharted territory.

As demographic fatigue sets in and the inability of governments to deal effectively with the consequences of rapid population growth becomes more evident, the resulting social stresses are likely to exacerbate conflicts among differing religious, ethnic, tribal, or geographic groups within societies. Among these are differences between Hindus and Moslems in India; Yorubas, Ibos, and Hausas in Nigeria; Arabs and Israelis in the Middle East; Hutus and Tutsis in Rwanda and Burundi; and many others. Aside from enormous social costs, these spreading conflicts could drive countless millions across national borders as they seek safety, putting pressure on industrial countries to admit them as political refugees.

As pressures on the Earth's resources build, they may also lead to international conflicts over shared water resources, oceanic fisheries, or other scarce resources. Nowhere is the potential conflict over scarce water more stark than among the three principal countries of the Nile River valley—Egypt, the Sudan, and Ethiopia. In Egypt, where it rarely rains, agriculture is almost wholly dependent on water from the Nile. Egypt now gets the lion's share of the Nile's water, but its current population of 66 million is projected to reach 115 million by 2050, thus greatly boosting the demand for grain, even without any gains in per capita consumption. The Sudan, whose population is projected to double from 29 million today to 60 million by 2050, also depends heavily on the Nile. The population of Ethiopia, the country that controls 85 percent of the headwaters of the Nile, is projected to expand from 62 million to 213 million. With little Nile water now reaching the Mediterranean, if either of the two upstream countries, Sudan or Ethiopia, use more water, Egypt will get less.[133]

After the political situation stabilized in Ethiopia, national attention turned to economic development and the government built 200 small dams. Although these are collectively taking only 500 million cubic meters of water out of the Nile's total flow of 85 billion cubic meters, the government plans to use much more of the Nile's water as it expands power generation and irrigation in the effort to lift its people out of poverty. With gross national product per person in Ethiopia averaging only $100 per year compared with $1,080 in Egypt, it is difficult to argue that the former should not use more of the Nile's water. As the collective population of these three countries expands by 231 million, going from 157 million at present to 388 million in 2050, it is simply outstripping the local supply of water. Although it is only one of the many potential conflicts that could be triggered as population pressures mount, this one—involving both Muslims and Christians—could destabilize the entire Middle East.[134]

As we look to the future, the challenge for world leaders is to help countries maximize the prospects for breaking out of stage two of the demographic transition and moving into stage three before time runs out and nature brutally forces them back into stage one. In a world where both grain output and fish catch per person are falling, a strong case can be made on humanitarian grounds for an all-out effort to stabilize world population. There is nothing inevitable about a projected mid-century population of 9.4 billion. We can choose to move to the lower trajectory of the three U.N.

FIGURE 12

World Population Projections Under Three Variants, 1950–2050

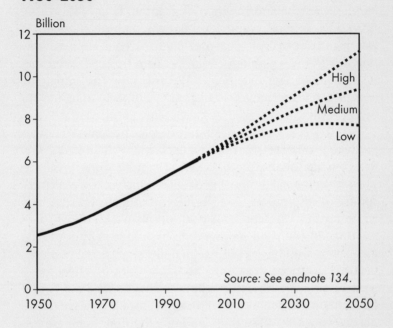

Source: See endnote 134.

projection scenarios, which has world population stabilizing at 7.7 billion by 2050. (See Figure 12.) This would reduce the number to be added by 2050 from 3.3 billion to a more manageable 1.7 billion.[135]

What is needed, to use a basketball term, is a full-court press—an all-out effort to lower fertility, particularly in the high-fertility countries, while there is still time. We see four key steps in doing this: undertaking national carrying capacity assessments to help governments and the public at large to better understand the urgency of stabilizing population, filling the family planning gap, educating young women, and adopting a worldwide campaign to stop at two surviving children.

Two hundred years ago, Thomas Malthus could only discuss the population-food relationship in general terms, but we now have enough information for each country to calculate with some confidence its population carrying capacity—the number of people that can be supported at the desired level of food consumption. We now know what the cropland area is and roughly what it will be a half-century from now. In most countries there will be little change. For water, current hydrological data give us a good sense of how much will be available for each country in 2050, assuming no major changes in climate. We also now can anticipate within a narrow range what grain yield potentials are for each country.

U.S. Department of Agriculture plant scientist Thomas R. Sinclair observes that advances in plant physiology now let scientists quantify crop yield potentials quite precisely. The physiological limits of such metabolic processes as transpiration, respiration, and photosynthesis are well known. He notes that "except for a few options which allow small increases in the yield ceiling, the physiological limit to crop yields may well have been reached under experimental conditions." In those situations, national or local, where farmers are using the highest-yielding varieties that plant breeders can provide and the agronomic inputs and practices needed to realize fully their genetic potential, there are few options left for dramatically raising land productivity.[136]

As noted earlier, the unprecedented worldwide rise in land productivity that began at mid-century has slowed dramatically since 1990, with no foreseeable prospect of a rapid rise being restored. In some of the more agriculturally advanced countries, yields are showing signs of plateauing. A lack of new technologies to raise land productivity is not the only constraint. As noted earlier, the world's farmers now face a continuing shrinkage in the cropland area per person, a steady shrinkage in irrigation water per person, and a diminishing crop yield response to the use of additional fertilizer.[137]

Given the limits to the carrying capacity of each country's land and water resources, every national government now needs a carefully articulated and adequately supported population policy, one that takes into account the country's carrying capacity at whatever consumption level citizens decide on. As Harvard biologist Edward O. Wilson observes in his landmark book *The Diversity of Life*, "Every nation has an economic policy and a foreign policy. The time has come to speak more openly of a population policy. By this I mean not just the capping of growth when the population hits the wall, as in China and India, but a policy based on a rational solution of this problem; what, in the judgment of its informed citizenry, is the *optimal* population?"[138]

As a starting point, governments can calculate their population carrying capacity by estimating the land available for crops, the amount of water that will be available for irrigation over the long term, and the likely yield of crops based on what the most advanced countries with similar growing conditions have achieved. Without such a calculation, many national governments are simply flying blind into the future, allowing their nations to drift into a world in which population growth and environmental degradation can lead to social disintegration. Once projections of future food supplies are completed, then societies can consider what combination of population size and consumption level they want, recognizing that there are tradeoffs between the two.

Governments of countries where the carrying capacity assessments show growing grain deficits may assume they can cover these with imports. But the projected growth in national grain deficits is collectively likely to far exceed exportable grain surpluses, which have increased little since 1980. (See Figure 13.) Even though the cropland held out of production under U.S. farm commodity programs over the last half-century was returned to use after these programs were dismantled in 1995, the United States—the world's leading grain exporter—has actually experienced some shrinkage in its exportable surplus in recent years as the growth in domestic demands has exceeded the growth in production.[139]

Filling the family planning gap—the second key step—is a high payoff area. In a world where population pressures

FIGURE 13

Grain Exports from Argentina, Australia, Canada, European Union, and the United States, 1960–98

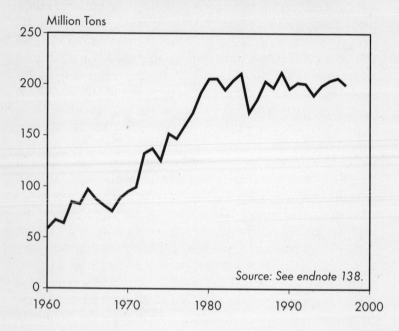

Source: See endnote 138.

are mounting, the inability of 120 million of the world's women to get family planning services is inexcusable. The International Conference on Population and Development held in Cairo in 1994 concluded that providing quality reproductive health services to all those in need in developing countries would cost about $17 billion in the year 2000. By 2015, this would climb to $22 billion. The agreement was for donor countries to provide one third of the funds, with the developing countries providing the remaining two thirds. Unfortunately, the industrial countries, most importantly the United States, have reneged on this commitment.[140]

Educating girls is a key to accelerating this shift to smaller families. In every society for which data are available, the more education women have, the fewer children they have. Closely related to the need for education of young females is the need to provide equal opportunities for women in all phases of national life.[141]

The challenge the world is facing with the population issue is both complex and demanding. At issue is whether we as a species can understand the consequences of continuing population growth and act quickly to slow it. Do we care enough about the world our children will live in to take action now? We regularly buy insurance to reduce uncertainty and to protect ourselves from future disasters, but there is no insurance policy that will pay greater dividends for the next generation than a modest investment in population stabilization today.

Above all, the world needs leadership on this issue. If we are facing a population emergency, it should be treated as such. It may be time for a campaign to convince couples everywhere to restrict their childbearing to replacement-level fertility. In his new book, *Maybe One: A Personal and Environmental Argument for Single-Child Families*, environmental writer Bill McKibben urges American couples to consider having only one child in order to slow population growth and buy time to regain control of our environmental destiny. Zero Population Growth, a U.S. nongovernmental organization, has long pushed for population stabilization in the United States. And in early 1998, the Baltimore chapter of the Sierra Club, a leading U.S. environmental group, went on record urging that couples limit the number of their surviving children to two. The time may have come for world leaders—the President of the United States, the Secretary-General of the United Nations, and the President of the World Bank, among others—to do the same.[142]

It may also be time for the world's wealthiest individuals, the 600 or so billionaires, to make a commitment to the global future as Ted Turner did when in September 1997 he pledged $1 billion to help the United Nations deal with problems such as population, environment, and health. It makes little sense for today's billionaires to argue that they will put their wealth in a foundation when they die, perhaps 20 or 30 years from now, when the commitments are needed now to ensure that our future world is a livable one. The problems we are facing as a species are not unmanageable unless we permit them to become so.[143]

We live in a demographically divided world—one that consists of countries that have reached or are approaching the stability of stage three of the demographic transition and countries where rising mortality is forcing them back into stage one. Despite this stark contrast, our world is environmentally interdependent and more economically integrated than ever before. In this integrated world, there are no longer "their problems" and "our problems." Only our problems.

Notes

1. All population data in this paper, including per capita calculations, are from United Nations, *World Population Prospects: The 1996 Revision* (New York: 1996) unless otherwise noted.

2. Thomas Robert Malthus, *An Essay on the Principle of Population (1798)*, from the Norton Critical Edition, ed. by Philip Appleman (New York: W.W. Norton & Company, 1976).

3. U.S. Department of Agriculture (USDA), *Production, Supply, and Distribution (PS&D)*, electronic database, Washington, DC, updated August 1998; USDA, "World Grain Database," unpublished printout, Washington, DC, 1991; U.N. Food and Agriculture Organization (FAO), *The Sixth World Food Survey* (Rome: 1996); U.S. Bureau of the Census, International Programs Center, "Historical Estimates of World Population," <http://www.census.gov/ipc/ www/worldhis.html>, 1998.

4. World Health Organization (WHO), "Child Malnutrition," Fact Sheet No. 119 (Geneva: November 1996); WHO, *The World Health Report 1998* (Geneva: 1998).

5. Table 1 from United Nations, op. cit. note 1.

6. U.S. Bureau of the Census, *International Data Base*, electronic database, Suitland, MD, updated 15 June 1998.

7. Population Reference Bureau (PRB), "1998 World Population Data Sheet," wall chart (Washington, DC: June 1998).

8. Ibid.

9. Table 2 from United Nations, op. cit. note 1.

10. Lumber from FAO, FAOSTAT, *Statistics Database*, <http://apps. fao.org>, viewed 5 August 1998; paper from International Institute for Environment and Development (IIED), *Towards a Sustainable Paper Cycle* (London: 1996) and from FAO, op. cit. this note; water from Sandra Postel, *Last Oasis*, rev. ed. (New York: W.W. Norton & Company, 1997); fossil fuels 1950–70 from United Nations, *World Energy Supplies 1950–74* (New York: 1976), and from United Nations, *Energy Statistics Yearbook* (New York: various years); fossil fuels 1970–95 from U.S. Department of Energy (DOE), Energy Information Administration (EIA), Office of Energy Markets and End Use, *International Statistics Database*, provided by Linda Doman at DOE, EIA, electronic communication, 5 August 1998; grain from USDA, *PS&D*, op. cit. note 3.

11. Alan Durning, *How Much Is Enough?* (New York: W.W. Norton & Company, 1992).

12. FAO, *The State of World Fisheries and Aquaculture, 1996* (Rome: 1997).

13. USDA, *PS&D*, op. cit. note 3.

14. Ajay Khudania, "India Struggles with Fading Water Supply," *Hindustan Times*, 20 July 1998.

15. International Labour Organisation (ILO), *World Employment 1996/97* (Geneva: 1997); ILO, *Economically Active Population, 1950–2010* (Geneva: 1997).

16. Figure 1 from USDA, *PS&D*, op. cit. note 3, and from USDA, "World Grain Database," op. cit. note 3.

17. USDA, *PS&D*, op. cit. note 3; USDA, "World Grain Database," op. cit. note 3.

18. USDA, *PS&D*, op. cit. note 3; USDA, "World Grain Database," op. cit. note 3.

19. FAO, op. cit. note 10.

20. Mark W. Rosegrant and Claudia Ringler, "World Food Markets into the 21st Century: Environmental and Resource Constraints and Policies," revision of a paper presented at the RIRDC-sponsored plenary session of the 41st Annual Conference of the Australian Agricultural and Resource Economics Society, Queensland, Australia, 22–25 January 1997; K.G. Soh and K.F. Isherwood, "Short Term Prospects for World Agriculture and Fertilizer Use," presentation at IFA Enlarged Council Meeting, International Fertilizer Industry Association, Monte Carlo, Monaco, 18–21 November 1997.

21. USDA, *PS&D*, op. cit. note 3.

22. Calculations based on current grain consumption per person in the United States and India from USDA, *PS&D*, op. cit. note 3.

23. USDA, *PS&D*, op. cit. note 3.

24. Postel, op. cit. note 10.

25. Ibid.; Wang Chengshan, "What Does the Yellow River Tell?" *Openings*, Winter 1997.

26. David Seckler, David Molded, and Randolph Barker, "Water Scarcity in the Twenty-First Century" (Colombo, Sri Lanka: International Water Management Institute (IWMI), 27 July 1998).

27. I.A. Shiklomanov, "World Fresh Water Resources," in Peter H. Gleick, ed., *Water in Crisis: A Guide to the World's Fresh Water Resources* (New York: Oxford University Press, 1993).

28. Figure of 1,000 tons of water for one ton of wheat from FAO, *Yield Response to Water* (Rome: 1979); "Water Scarcity as a Key Factor Behind Global Food Insecurity: Round Table Discussion," *Ambio*, March 1998.

29. Nile flow from Sandra Postel, *Dividing the Waters: Food Security, Ecosystem Health, and the New Politics of Scarcity*, Worldwatch Paper 132 (Washington, DC: Worldwatch Institute, September 1996); USDA, *PS&D*, op. cit. note 3.

30. Figure 2 from FAO, op. cit. note 10; Sandra Postel, "Water for Food Production: Will There Be Enough in 2025?" *BioScience*, August 1998.

31. Seckler, Molded, and Barker, op. cit. note 26.

32. Extinction rates from Chris Bright, *Life Out of Bounds* (New York: W.W. Norton & Company, 1998); species loss factors from John Tuxill and Chris Bright, "Losing Strands in the Web of Life," in Lester R. Brown et al., *State of the World 1998* (New York: W.W. Norton & Company, 1998).

33. Jonathan Baillie and Brian Groombridge, eds., *1996 IUCN Red List of Threatened Animals* (Gland, Switzerland: World Conservation Union–IUCN, 1996); Table 3 from Tuxill and Bright, op. cit. note 32.

34. Population concentration and migration estimates from Don Hinrichsen, *Coastal Waters of the World: Trends, Threats, and Strategies* (Washington, DC: Island Press, 1998); fisheries density from Peter Weber, "It Comes Down to the Coasts," *World Watch*, March/April 1994.

35. Habitat loss trends from Paul Harrison, *The Third Revolution* (New York: Penguin Books, 1992); biodiversity hotspots from Conservation International, "Global Biodiversity Hotspots," <http//www.conservation.org>; Table 4 is a Worldwatch calculation based on land area from FAO, *1996 Production Yearbook* (Rome: 1996) and on habitat loss from Harrison, op. cit. this note, and contains averages for countries at various levels of population density.

36. Extinction causes from Chris Bright, "Tracking the Ecology of Climate Change," in Lester R. Brown et al., *State of the World 1997* (New York: W.W. Norton & Company, 1997); impact of exotics from Bright, op. cit. note 32.

37. Peter M. Vitousek et al., "Human Alteration of the Global Nitrogen Cycle: Causes and Consequences," *Ecological Issues*, February 1997.

38. Ecological shift from Bright, op. cit. note 36.

39. Figure 3, for 1950–95, from G. Marland et al., "Global, Regional, and

National CO_2 Emission Estimates from Fossil Fuel Burning, Cement Production, and Gas Flaring: 1751–1995 (revised January 9, 1998)," Oak Ridge National Laboratory, <http://cdiac.esd.ornl.gov/>, viewed 14 August 1998; atmospheric carbon dioxide levels from C. D. Keeling and T. P. Whorf, "Atmospheric CO_2 Concentrations (ppmv) Derived from In Situ Air Samples Collected at Mauna Loa Observatory, Hawaii, 1958–1997 (revised August 1998)," Scripps Institute of Oceanography, <http://cdiac.esd.ornl.gov/>, viewed 14 August 1998; Figure 4 from James Hansen et al., Goddard Institute for Space Studies, Surface Air Temperature Analyses, "Global Land-Ocean Temperature Index," <http://www.giss.nasa.gov/Data/GISTEMP>, viewed 14 August 1998.

40. Carbon emissions 1995–2020 interpolated based on figures for each five-year period from DOE, EIA, *International Energy Outlook 1998, April 1998* (Washington, DC: 1998); carbon emissions 2020–50 use DOE's EIA figure for 2020 as the baseline year and growth rates for regional and global carbon emissions from 2020 to 2050 based on scenario IS92a in Robert T. Watson et al., eds., *Climate Change 1995: Impacts, Adaptations and Mitigation of Climate Change: Scientific-Technical Analyses: Contribution of Working Group II to the Second Assessment Report of the Intergovernmental Panel on Climate Change* (IPCC) (New York: Cambridge University Press, 1996); J.T. Houghton et al., "Stabilization of Atmospheric Greenhouse Gases: Physical, Biological and Socio-economic Implications," technical paper of the IPCC, February 1997.

41. Carbon emissions 1995–2020 from DOE, op. cit. note 40; carbon emissions 2020–50 based on Watson et al., op. cit. note 40.

42. Carbon emissions 1995–2020 from DOE, op. cit. note 40; carbon emissions 2020–50 based on Watson et al., op. cit. note 40.

43. Carbon emissions 1995–2020 from DOE, op. cit. note 40; carbon emissions 2020–50 based on Watson et al., op. cit. note 40.

44. Marland et al., op. cit. note 39; carbon emissions 1995–2020 from DOE, op. cit. note 40; carbon emissions 2020–50 based on Watson et al., op. cit. note 40.

45. Sandra Brown et al., "Management of Forests for Mitigation of Greenhouse Gas Emissions," in Watson et al., op. cit. note 40; Richard A. Houghton, "Converting Terrestrial Ecosystems from Sources to Sinks of Carbon," *Ambio*, June 1996; carbon from Asian fires from Sander Thoenes, "In Asia's Big Haze, Man Battles Man-Made Disaster," *Christian Science Monitor*, 28 October 1997.

46. Figure 5 from FAO, *Yearbook of Fishery Statistics: Catches and Landings* (Rome: various years), with 1990–96 data from FAO, Rome, letters to Worldwatch, 5 and 11 November 1997.

47.   FAO, op. cit. note 12.

48.   World's major fishing areas excludes inland catches and Antarctic waters. Eleven of 15 based on data from Maurizio Perotti, fishery statistician, Fishery Information, Data and Statistics Unit, Fisheries Department, FAO, Rome, e-mail to Worldwatch, 14 October 1997; Atlantic cod from S.M. Garcia and C. Newton, "Current Situation, Trends, and Prospects in World Fisheries," in E.K. Pikitch, D.D. Huppert, and M.P. Sissenwine, *Global Trends: Fisheries Management*, American Fisheries Society (AFS) Symposium 20 (Bethesda, MD: AFS, 1997); bluefin tuna from Lisa Speer et al., *Hook, Line and Sinking: The Crisis in Marine Fisheries* (New York: Natural Resources Defense Council, February 1997).

49.   FAO, *Yearbook*, op. cit. note 46.

50.   Price of tuna from "Bluefin Tuna Reported on Brink of Extinction," *Journal of Commerce*, 11 October 1993.

51.   Fisheries disputes from Johnathon Friedland, "Fish Stories These Days Are Tales of Deception and Growing Rivalry," *Wall Street Journal*, 25 November 1997; Greenpeace quote from William Branigin, "Global Accord Puts Curbs on Fishing," *Washington Post*, 4 August 1995.

52.   American Sportfishing Association and Ocean Wildlife Campaign, "Slaughter at Sea," press release (Washington, DC: 12 January 1998); Dayton L. Alverson et al., *A Global Assessment of Fisheries Bycatch and Discards*, FAO Fisheries Technical Paper 339 (Rome: FAO, 1994).

53.   Data for 1984–85 from FAO, *Aquaculture Production Statistics, 1984–1993*, FAO Fisheries Circular No. 815, Revision 7 (Rome: 1995); data for 1986–95 from FAO, *Aquaculture Production Statistics, 1986–1995*, FAO Fisheries Circular No. 815, Revision 9 (Rome: 1997); data for 1996–97 from Maurizio Perotti, fishery statistician, Fishery Information, Data and Statistics Unit, Fisheries Department, FAO, Rome, letter to Worldwatch, 11 November 1997.

54.   FAO, *Yearbook*, op. cit. note 46; 1990–96 data from FAO, letters, op. cit. note 46.

55.   ILO, *Economically Active Population,* op cit. note 15; ILO, *World Employment 1996/97*, op cit. note 15; Michael Hopkins, "A Global Look at Jobless Growth, Poverty, and Unemployment: Trends and Future Prospects," prepared for ILO, September 1994; labor force projections are based on U.N. projections of population and dependency ratios and ILO projections of regional work activity rates for the year 2000.

56.   Indermit S. Gill and Amit Dar, *Labor Market Policies and Interventions for Sustainable Employment Growth* (draft) (Washington, DC: World Bank, 7 September 1994); Table 5 from U.N. projections of population and depen-

dency ratios and ILO projections of regional work activity rates for the year 2000.

57. ILO, "Labour Supply and Employment," *Spotlight* (newsletter of the Labour and Population Programme), December 1997.

58. ILO, *Jobs for Africa: A Policy Framework for an Employment-Intensive Growth Strategy* (Geneva: August 1997); poverty is defined here as surviving on less than $1 per person per day; labor force projections are based on UN projections of population and dependency ratios and ILO projections of regional work activity rates for the year 2000; additional background from ILO, op. cit. note 58.

59. World Bank, *Claiming the Future: Choosing Prosperity in the Middle East and North Africa* (Washington, DC: 1995); unemployment data for Algeria from Roger Cohen, "In Algeria, Oil and Islam Make a Volatile Mixture," *New York Times*, 28 December 1996; growth in labor force from ILO, *Economically Active Population*, op. cit. note 15.

60. Labor force projections are based on UN projections of population and dependency ratios and ILO projections of regional work activity rates for the year 2000; Judy Pehrson, "Disgruntled Chinese Worker Miss the 'Iron Rice Bowl'," *Christian Science Monitor*, 13 March 1998; Edmond Lococo, "China Feed, Livestock Mid-year Update," *Bridge News*, 30 June 1998; Associated Press, "China Fires 3¹/₂ Million Government Employees," *San Francisco Examiner*, 10 August 1998; John Pomfret, "Workers and Reforms Fall into 'China's Slump'," *Washington Post*, 11 August 1998.

61. UNICEF, *The Progress of Nations* (New York: Oxford University Press, 1997); ILO, *World Employment 1996/97*, op. cit. note 15.

62. Grainland data from USDA, *PS&D*, op. cit. note 3; A.S. Oberai, *Population Growth, Employment and Poverty in Third-World Mega-Cities* (New York: St. Martin's Press, 1993).

63. Nancy Birdsall, "Government, Population, and Poverty: A Win-Win Tale," in Robert Cassen, ed., *Population and Development: Old Debates, New Conclusions* (New Brunswick, NJ: Transaction Publishers, 1994); Erik Eckholm, "China Jobless Fuel a Growth Industry," *New York Times*, 31 May 1998; Jeremy Rifkin and Robert L. Heilbroner, *The End of Work* (New York: Putnam, 1996); Steven Greenhouse, "The Relentless March of Labor's True Foe," *New York Times*, 2 August 1998.

64. ILO, *World Employment 1996/97*, op. cit. note 15.

65. Grain area from USDA, *PS&D*, op. cit. note 3.

66. Faltering grain yields from Lester R. Brown, "Can We Raise Grain Yields Fast Enough?" *World Watch*, July/August 1997.

67. Figure 6 from USDA, *PS&D*, op, cit. note 3.

68. Grain area from USDA, *PS&D*, op. cit. note 3; 1950 grain area from USDA, "World Grain Database," op. cit. note 3.

69. Grain area from USDA, *PS&D*, op. cit. note 3.

70. Ibid.

71. Erosion from Per Pinstrup Andersen and Rajul Pandya-Lorch, "Alleviating Poverty, Intensifying Agriculture, and Effectively Managing Natural Resources," Food, Agriculture, and the Environment Discussion Paper 1 (Washington, DC: International Food Policy Research Institute, 1994); fallow periods from Joy Tivy, *Agricultural Ecology* (Essex, UK: Longman Scientific and Technical, 1990).

72. Landlessness from United Nations, *Government Views on the Relationships between Population and Environment* (New York: United Nations, Department of Economic and Social Affairs, 1997).

73. Table 6 based on population from Bureau of Census, op. cit. note 3, and on forested area from Alan Durning, "Redesigning the Forest Economy," in Lester R. Brown et al., *State of the World 1994* (New York: W.W. Norton & Company, 1994).

74. Latin American deforestation factors from Harrison, op. cit. note 35; meat consumption from USDA, *PS&D*, op. cit. note 3; world deforestation factors from Dirk Bryant, Daniel Nielsen, and Laura Tangley, *The Last Frontier Forests: Ecosystems and Economies on the Edge* (Washington, DC: World Resources Institute, 1997); fuelwood consumption to population growth correlation from FAO, *Regional Study on Wood Energy Today and Tomorrow in Asia* (Bangkok: 1997).

75. Paper and paperboard use from FAO, op. cit. note 10.

76. Current consumption from FAO, op. cit. note 10; projected consumption based on ibid.

77. Sustainable estimates and growth predictions from Duncan McLaren et al., *Tomorrow's World: Britain's Share in a Sustainable Future* (London: Earthscan Publications, 1998). McLaran's analysis is updated using FAO data for industrial roundwood for 1996.

78. Forest services from Norman Myers, "The World's Forests and Their Ecosystem Services," in Gretchen C. Daily, ed., *Nature's Services: Societal Dependence on Natural Ecosystems* (Washington, DC: Island Press, 1997); carbon from deforestation from Houghton, op. cit. note 45.

79. United Nations Centre for Human Settlements (HABITAT), *An*

Urbanizing World: Global Report on Human Settlements, 1996 (Oxford, UK: Oxford University Press, 1996); Worldwatch housing projections are based on U.N. population projections and household size for 1995 from ibid., assuming a 15-percent reduction in number of people per household by 2050.

80. Table 7 contains Worldwatch housing projections based on UN population projections and household size for 1995 from HABITAT, op. cit. note 79, assuming a 15-percent reduction in number of people per household by 2050.

81. Worldwatch projections.

82. HABITAT, op. cit. note 79.

83. Ibid.; Erik Eckholm, "A Burst of Renewal Sweeps Old Beijing Into the Dumpsters," *New York Times*, 1 March 1998; Michael Janofsky, "Shortage of Housing for Poor Grows in US," *New York Times*, 28 April 1998.

84. Floor space per person from Gopal Ahluwalia, National Association of Home Builders, Washington, DC, discussion with author, 17 August 1998; HABITAT op. cit. note 79.

85. UNICEF, op. cit. note 62; HABITAT, op. cit. note 79.

86. UNICEF, op. cit. note 62; HABITAT, op. cit. note 79; Martin Brockerhoff and Ellen Brennan, "The Poverty of Cities in Developing Regions," *Population and Development Review*, March 1998; Oberai, op. cit. note 63.

87. Figure 7 and discussion based on the following: energy use 1950–70 based on historic world oil, natural gas, hydroelectric, and coal use from United Nations, *World Energy Supplies 1950–74*, op. cit. note 10, and from United Nations, *Energy Statistics Yearbook*, op. cit. note 10; energy use 1970–95 from DOE, op. cit. note 10; energy use 1995–2020 interpolated based on figures for each five-year period from DOE, op. cit. note 40; energy use 2020–50 uses DOE's EIA figure for 2020 as the baseline year and growth rates for regional and global energy use from 2020 to 2050 based on scenario "IS92a" in Watson et al., op. cit. note 40.

88. World oil production from United Nations, *World Energy Supplies 1950–74*, op. cit. note 10, and from DOE, op. cit. note 10; oil production projections from Jean Laherrere, Petroconsultants, Geneva, Switzerland, electronic communication, 12 July 1998; oil production projections from IPCC, provided by Jae Edmonds, electronic communication, 30 July 1998; Colin J. Campbell and Jean H. Laherrere, "The End of Cheap Oil," *Scientific American*, March 1998.

89. World Bank, *Rural Energy and Development: Improving Energy Supplies for*

Two Billion People (Washington, DC: 1996).

90. Table 8 from United Nations, *World Urbanization Prospects: 1996 Revision* (New York: 1997); U.N. projections only go to 2030, figures for 2040–50 are Worldwatch extrapolations.

91. London figure from Andrew Lees, *Cities Perceived: Urban Society in European and American Thought: 1820–1940* (New York: Columbia University Press, 1985); United Nations, op. cit. note 90.

92. United Nations, op. cit. note 90.

93. Ibid.

94. Brockerhoff and Brennan, op. cit. note 86.

95. IUCN, *Protected Areas and Demographic Change: Planning for the Future,* proceedings of the IVth World Congress on National Parks and Protected Areas, Caracas, Venezuela, 10–21 February 1992 (Gland, Switzerland: Burlington Press, 1992).

96. Sunil Sampat, Bombay, India, e-mail to author, 15 May 1998; Juan Manuel Martinez Valdez, ECOPOL (Ecologia y Poblacion), Mexico City, personal communication, 10 May 1998; IUCN, "Las Areas Naturales Protegidas de la Argentina" (Buenos Aries, January 1998); Table 9 from A. de Sherbinin, *Population Dynamics and Protected Areas: Options for Action,* IUCN Issues in Social Policy (Gland, Switzerland: forthcoming), from Ministry of Tourism and Civil Aviation, Department of Tourism, *Annual Statistical Report 1996* (Kathmandu, Nepal: 1996), from Alan Mairson, "The Everglades: Dying for Help," *National Geographic,* April 1994, from Kevin Collins, National Parks and Conservation Association, discussion with author, 29 April 1998, from "Recreational Golf in the US," *Christian Science Monitor,* 9 April 1998, from Edwin Moure, Biscayne National Park, Florida, discussion with author, 2 August 1998, and from "Sugar's Latest Everglades Threat," *New York Times,* 29 April 1998.

97. Stan Stevens, "The Legacy of Yellowstone," in Stan Stevens, ed., *Conservation Through Cultural Survival: Indigenous People and Protected Areas* (Washington, DC: Island Press, 1997).

98. De Sherbinin, op. cit. note 96; Ministry of Tourism and Civil Aviation, op. cit. note 96.

99. De Sherbinin, op. cit. note 96.

100. Collins, op. cit. note 96; "Sugar's Latest Everglades Threat," op. cit. note 96.

101. Hinrichsen, op. cit. note 34.

102. Farah Gadgil, Bombay Environmental Action Group, Bombay, India, e-mail to author, 4 May 1998; Betty Spence, "Getting Along With the Elephants," *Christian Science Monitor*, 11 February 1998; James C. McKinley Jr., "It's Kenya's Farmers vs. Wildlife, and the Animals are Losing," *New York Times*, 2 August 1998.

103. Douglas Martin, "On City's Playing Fields, a Turf War," *New York Times*, 5 April 1998; United Nations, op. cit. note 90; U.S. National Park Service, <http://www.nps.gov/planning/yosemite/vip/fact/f01.htm>; Tom Kenworthy, "The Cost of the Wild," *Washington Post*, 10 August 1997; Associated Press, "Congress Moving to Extend Park Fees, Despite Protests," *Washington Post*, 10 August 1998.

104. Figure 8 and Table 10 from United Nations, op. cit. note 1.

105. Current student-teacher ratio is an average taken from U.N. Development Programme (UNDP), *Human Development Report 1996* (New York: Oxford University Press, 1996), which uses data from 1992; African education statistics from Fay Chung, "Education in Africa Today," in Jacques Delor, *Learning: the Treasure Within*, report to UNESCO of the International Commission on Education for the Twenty-First Century (Paris: UNESCO, 1996).

106. UNESCO benchmark from Delor, op. cit. note 105; education investment from UNDP, op. cit. note 105.

107. Waste volume estimates from William Rathje and Cullen Murphy, *Rubbish! The Archaeology of Garbage* (New York: Harper Collins, 1992); international waste production data from International Maritime Organization (IMO), *Global Waste Survey Final Report* (London: 1995); Table 11 based on the following: average municipal solid waste generation rates from U.S. Environmental Protection Agency, *Characterization of Municipal Solid Waste* (Washington, DC: 1995), and from Roger Pfammeter and Roland Schertenleib, "Non-Governmental Refuse Collection in Low-Income Urban Areas," SANDEC Report No. 1/96 (Duebenborf, Switzerland: Swiss Federal Institute for Environmental Science and Technology, Department of Water and Sanitation in Developing Countries, March 1996); volume of plastic from Rathje and Murphy, op. cit. this note; IMO data from IMO, op. cit. this note; sanitation from WHO, Water Supply and Sanitation Collaborative Council, and UNICEF, *Water Supply and Sanitation Sector Monitoring Report, 1996* (New York: WHO, 1996), and from UNICEF, op. cit. note 62.

108. Waste production data and correlation to economic level from OECD, *OECD Environmental Data 1995* (Paris: 1995), and from Pfammeter and Schertenleib, op. cit. note 107. OECD lists municipal waste per capita for member countries as 500 kilos per person for 1992. Using more update population figures, we calculate per capita generation to be some 442 kilos per person in 1990. Data for developing countries are scarce, but using the commonly cited figure of half a kilo per person per day, their citizens would

generate 183 kilos per year.

109. Access to sanitation from WHO, Water Supply and Sanitation Collaborative Council, and UNICEF, op. cit. note 107 (based on a survey of 84 of 130 developing countries, not including Eastern Europe or Central Asia), and from UNICEF, op. cit. note 62; disease incidence from WHO, "Water and Sanitation," Fact Sheet No. 112 (Geneva: November 1996); diarrhea mortality from UNICEF, op. cit. note 62.

110. Rural sanitation shortage and future sanitation requirements from WHO, Water Supply and Sanitation Collaborative Council, and UNICEF, op. cit. note 107; urban sanitation impacts from UNICEF, op. cit. note 62; 3 billion is a Worldwatch estimate based on United Nations, op. cit. note 90.

111. Statistics from WHO, Water Supply and Sanitation Collaborative Council, and UNICEF, op. cit. note 106.

112. Figure 9 from FAO, *1948–1985 World Crop and Livestock Statistics* (Rome: 1987), from FAO, *FAO Production Yearbooks 1988–1991* (Rome: 1990–93), and from USDA, Foreign Agricultural Service, *Livestock and Poultry: World Markets and Trade*, March 1998.

113. FAO, *Crop and Livestock Statistics*, op. cit. note 112; FAO, *Production Yearbooks*, op. cit. note 112; USDA, op. cit. note 112.

114. FAO, *Crop and Livestock Statistics*, op. cit. note 112; FAO, *Production Yearbooks*, op. cit. note 112; USDA, op. cit. note 112; grain-to-poultry ratio derived from Robert V. Bishop et al., *The World Poultry Market—Government Intervention and Multilateral Policy Reform* (Washington, DC: USDA, 1990); grain-to-pork ratio from Leland Southard, Livestock and Poultry Situation and Outlook Staff, Economic Research Service (ERS), USDA, Washington, DC, discussion with Worldwatch, 27 April 1992; grain-to-beef ratio based on Allen Baker, Feed Situation and Outlook Staff, ERS, USDA, Washington, DC, discussion with Worldwatch, 27 April 1992.

115. USDA, *PS&D*, op. cit. note 3.

116. Ibid.

117. Ibid.

118. Ibid.; idled land from USDA, Economic Research Service, "AREI Updates: Cropland Use in 1997," No. 5 (Washington, DC: 1997).

119. Gross world product data for 1950 and 1955 from Herbert R. Block, *The Planetary Product in 1980: A Creative Pause?* (Washington, DC: U.S. Department of State, 1981), from International Monetary Fund (IMF), *World Economic Outlook*, May 1998 (Washington, DC: 1998), and from IMF,

International Financial Statistics (Washington, DC: various years).

120. Figure 10 based on Block, op. cit. note 119, on IMF, *World Economic Outlook*, op. cit. note 119, and on IMF, *International Financial Statistics*, op. cit. note 119.

121. World Bank, *Global Development Finance, 1998* (Washington, DC: 1998).

122. World Bank, *Food Security for the World*, statement prepared for the World Food Summit by the World Bank, 12 November 1996.

123. Frank Notestein, "Population—The Long View," in P.W. Schultz, ed., *Food for The World* (University of Chicago Press: 1945); Warren Thompson, "Population," *American Journal of Sociology*, vol. 34, no. 6, 1929.

124. Table 12 from PRB, op. cit. note 7.

125. Figure 11 from ibid., and from USDA, *PS&D*, op. cit. note 3; Rosegrant and Ringler, op. cit. note 20.

126. Table 13 from United Nations, op. cit. note 1, and from PRB, op. cit. note 7; Tom Gardner-Outlaw and Robert Engelman, *Sustaining Water, Easing Scarcity (A Second Update)* (Washington, DC: Population Action International, 1997).

127. Joint United Nations Programme on HIV/AIDS (UNAIDS) and WHO, *Report on the Global HIV/AIDS Epidemic* (Geneva: June 1998); Lawrence K. Altman, "Parts of Africa Showing H.I.V. In 1 in 4 Adults," *New York Times*, 24 June 1998.

128. Michael Specter, "Doctors Powerless as AIDS Rakes Africa," *Washington Post*, 6 August 1998.

129. UNAIDS and WHO, op. cit. note 127.

130. USDA, *PS&D*, op. cit. note 3.

131. Seckler, Molded, and Barker, op. cit. note 26.

132. USDA, *PS&D*, op. cit. note 3.

133. Postel, op. cit. note 10.

134. Gardner-Outlaw and Engelman, op. cit. note 126; PRB, op. cit. note 7.

135. Figure 12 from United Nations, op. cit. note 1.

136. Thomas R. Sinclair, "Limits to Crop Yield?" in American Society of

Agronomy, Crop Science Society of America, and Soil Science Society of America, *Physiology and Determination of Crop Yield* (Madison, WI: 1994).

137. USDA, *PS&D*, op. cit. note 3; Rosegrant and Ringler, op. cit. note 20.

138. Edward O. Wilson, *The Diversity of Life* (New York: WW Norton & Company, 1993).

139. Figure 13 from USDA, *PS&D*, op. cit. note 3.

140. "Broken Promises: U.S. Public Funding for International and Domestic Reproductive Health Care" (draft), prepared by the Mobilizing Resources Task Force, U.S. NGOs in Support of the Cairo Consensus, Washington, DC, 15 July 1998.

141. Nancy E. Riley, "Gender, Power, and Population Change," *Population Bulletin*, May 1997.

142. Bill McKibben, *Maybe One: A Personal and Environmental Argument for Single-Child Families* (New York: Simon & Schuster, 1998); Baltimore Chapter, Sierra Club, pamphlet on population, February 1998.

143. David Rohde, "Ted Turner Plans a $1 Billion Gift for U.N. Agencies," *New York Times*, 19 November 1997.

Worldwatch Papers

No. of Copies

Worldwatch Papers by Lester R. Brown or Gary Gardner

_____143. **Beyond Malthus: Sixteen Dimensions of the Population Problem**
by Lester R. Brown, Gary Gardner, and Brian Halweil

_____136. **The Agricultural Link: How Environmental Deterioration Could Disrupt Economic Progress** by Lester R. Brown

_____135. **Recycling Organic Waste: From Urban Pollutant to Farm Resource** by Gary Gardner

_____131. **Shrinking Fields: Cropland Loss in a World of Eight Billion** by Gary Gardner

_____142. **Rocking the Boat: Conserving Fisheries and Protecting Jobs** by Anne Platt McGinn

_____141. **Losing Strands in the Web of Life: Vertebrate Declines and the Conservation of Biological Diversity** by John Tuxill

_____140. **Taking a Stand: Cultivating a New Relationship with the World's Forests**
by Janet N. Abramovitz

_____139. **Investing in the Future: Harnessing Private Capital Flows for Environmentally Sustainable Development** by Hilary F. French

_____138. **Rising Sun, Gathering Winds: Policies to Stabilize the Climate and Strengthen Economies** by Christopher Flavin and Seth Dunn

_____137. **Small Arms, Big Impact: The Next Challenge of Disarmament** by Michael Renner

_____134. **Getting the Signals Right: Tax Reform to Protect the Environment and the Economy**
by David Malin Roodman

_____133. **Paying the Piper: Subsidies, Politics, and the Environment** by David Malin Roodman

_____132. **Dividing the Waters: Food Security, Ecosystem Health, and the New Politics of Scarcity** by Sandra Postel

_____130. **Climate of Hope: New Strategies for Stabilizing the World's Atmosphere**
by Christopher Flavin and Odil Tunali

_____129. **Infecting Ourselves: How Environmental and Social Disruptions Trigger Disease** by Anne E. Platt

_____128. **Imperiled Waters, Impoverished Future: The Decline of Freshwater Ecosystems**
by Janet N. Abramovitz

_____127. **Eco-Justice: Linking Human Rights and the Environment** by Aaron Sachs

_____126. **Partnership for the Planet: An Environmental Agenda for the United Nations**
by Hilary F. French

_____125. **The Hour of Departure: Forces That Create Refugees and Migrants** by Hal Kane

_____124. **A Building Revolution: How Ecology and Health Concerns Are Transforming Construction** by David Malin Roodman and Nicholas Lenssen

_____123. **High Priorities: Conserving Mountain Ecosystems and Cultures**
by Derek Denniston

_____122. **Budgeting for Disarmament: The Costs of War and Peace** by Michael Renner

_____121. **The Next Efficiency Revolution: Creating a Sustainable Materials Economy**
by John E. Young and Aaron Sachs

_____120. **Net Loss: Fish, Jobs, and the Marine Environment** by Peter Weber

_____119. **Powering the Future: Blueprint for a Sustainable Electricity Industry**
by Christopher Flavin and Nicholas Lenssen

_____118. **Back on Track: The Global Rail Revival** by Marcia D. Lowe

_____117. **Saving the Forests: What Will It Take?** by Alan Thein Durning

_____116. **Abandoned Seas: Reversing the Decline of the Oceans** by Peter Weber

_____115. **Global Network: Computers in a Sustainable Society** by John E. Young

_____114. **Critical Juncture: The Future of Peacekeeping** by Michael Renner

_____113. **Costly Tradeoffs: Reconciling Trade and the Environment** by Hilary F. French

_____110. **Gender Bias: Roadblock to Sustainable Development** by Jodi L. Jacobson

_____**Total copies (transfer number to order form on next page)**

PUBLICATION ORDER FORM

_____ *State of the World:* $13.95
The annual book used by journalists, activists, scholars, and policymakers worldwide to get a clear picture of the environmental problems we face.

_____ **Worldwatch Library: $30.00 (international subscribers $45)**
Receive *State of the World* and all six Worldwatch Papers as they are released during the calendar year.

_____ *Vital Signs:* $12.00
The book of trends that are shaping our future in easy to read graph and table format, with a brief commentary on each trend.

_____ **WORLD WATCH magazine subscription: $20.00 (international airmail $35.00)**
Stay abreast of global environmental trends and issues with our award-winning, eminently readable bimonthly magazine.

_____ **Worldwatch Database Disk Subscription: $89.00**
Contains global agricultural, energy, economic, environmental, social, and military indicators from all current Worldwatch publications including this Paper. Includes a mid-year update, and *Vital Signs* and *State of the World* as they are published. Can be used with Lotus 1-2-3, Quattro Pro, Excel, SuperCalc and many other spreadsheets.
Check one: _____ **IBM-compatible** _____ **Macintosh**

_____ **Worldwatch Papers—See list on previous page**
Single copy: $5.00
2–5: $4.00 ea. • 6–20: $3.00 ea. • 21 or more: $2.00 ea.

$4.00* Shipping and Handling *($8.00 outside North America)*
    minimum charge for S&H; call (800) 555-2028 for bulk order S&H

_____ **TOTAL** (U.S. dollars only)

Make check payable to Worldwatch Institute

1776 Massachusetts Ave., NW, Washington, DC 20036-1904 USA

Enclosed is my check or purchase order for U.S. $_____

☐ AMEX ☐ VISA ☐ MasterCard _____
                                      Card Number   Expiration Date

signature

name   **daytime phone #**

address

city   **state**   **zip/country**

phone: (800) 555-2028   fax: (202) 296-7365   e-mail: wwpub@worldwatch.org
website: www.worldwatch.org

Wish to make a tax-deductible contribution? Contact Worldwatch to find out how your donation can help advance our work.